$8.95
Q



# FATHER JOSEPH WRESINSKI

# FATHER JOSEPH WRESINSKI
## Voice of the Poorest

**by Alwine de Vos van Steenwijk**

Translated by Charles Sleeth

Queenship
**PUBLISHING COMPANY**
P.O Box 42028 Santa Barbara, CA 93140-2028
(800) 647-9882 • (805) 957-4893 • Fax: (805) 957-1631

To you, families of the Fourth World,
who teach us Father Joseph.



Library of Congress Number # 96-70126

Published by:
Queenship Publishing
P.O. Box 42028
Santa Barbara, CA 93140-2028
(800) 647-9882 • (805) 957-4893 • Fax: (805) 957-1631

Printed in the United States of America

ISBN: 1-882972-81-3

# TABLE OF CONTENTS

He dared to live with us the future that human beings are dreaming of, even when we were not yet able to fathom it ourselves... By refusing to abandon his own, he truly made the poorest of the poor his people. But then, all human beings, rich and poor of all creeds, became equally essential to him.

– Alwine de Vos van Steenwijk

# ACKNOWLEDGMENTS

We gratefully acknowledge Etienne de Ghellinck, Romy Hoffmann, Didier Robert and Françoise Vedrenne for their painstaking collaboration.

We also thank Father Théophane Chary and Monsignor Charles Molette, both for the attention they devoted to this book and for the indulgence they showed the author.

# PREFACE

As an African-American Bishop who has experienced poverty and exclusion growing up in Louisiana in the 20's and 30's, having worked with the poor all of my life as priest and missionary, I am most happy to introduce to the United States and the English-speaking world this biography of Father Joseph Wresinski.

Father Joseph came from the depth of deprivation even the majority of the world's poor are not necessarily condemned to suffer. It was among a "part of humanity living 'below sea level'" as he called it, that he started a movement which rapidly extended to all continents.

The Fourth World Movement is indeed a rare venture. Who else among the historical figures who have led humanity to join up with the poor has ever done so coming from where Joseph Wresinski came? He moved upwards with his people from the depths of society where few had ever succeeded in penetrating.

"All my life, I dreamed of restoring the very poor to the Church." The present biography tells us how Father Joseph realized this dream, convinced as he was that giving priority to the most deprived constituted the best guarantee that all human beings would thenceforth be respected in their community, their society, their Church.

Coming from extreme poverty himself, Father Joseph was in a unique position to bear witness to the fact that, in spite of our worldwide conviction to the contrary, the very poor are our equals, equally inhabited by the Spirit and capable of acting for the benefit of all. With them, he created the means allowing them to demonstrate that they are in fact the first defenders of human rights, the first agents of justice and peace, the first "experts in humanity," as he calls them.

The Volunteer Corps Father Joseph founded is a group of men and women dedicating their lives and skills to rebuilding self-confidence in others in areas of extreme poverty around the world.

Alwine de Vos van Steenwijk, the author of this book, is one of them, having lived and worked beside him for 28 years. With her help, Father Joseph also founded a body of supporters from all social, cultural, political and religious backgrounds, willing to put an end to extreme poverty. Unity among mankind was Father Joseph's passion which led him to "cast out his net in deep waters" far outside the secure walls of the Church he so deeply loved. His constant desire was that all people, whatever their spiritual background, would get a chance to share in her vocation to stand and suffer and hope with the very poorest.

Father Joseph and the Fourth World Movement these past thirty-eight years have demonstrated that very poor families, long-term Volunteers and supporters working together can produce significant results. Particularly, the Fourth World Movement has created a space where everyone can work together to end persistent poverty. The International Fourth World Family Congress held in New York and Washington in October 1994 was an example of this.

May this translation of the life and work of Father Joseph hasten the day of unity with and around those who throughout all continents are held in absolute deprivation. That is my prayer and the prayer, I am sure, of all people of good will. Such prayers, united to "the cries of the poor," are always heard, so the Scriptures say.

Bishop Leonard J. Olivier, S.V.D., D.D.
Auxiliary Bishop of Washington, D.C.

# INTRODUCTION

"Enfold our hope in their hope,
our love in their love,
our prayer in their prayers."

*Father Joseph Wresinski*

Beginning to tell Father Joseph's story means that we are promising one another not to put our pens down ever again. In this first book we will be speaking within the circle of Fourth World families, long-term Volunteers,[1] and friends.

This will not yet be a full-scale biography and we are not going to develop specific themes in it. Very simply, we are going to tell the story of the man whom we love and who has changed our lives. We are only beginning to understand all that he has given to us, only beginning to learn how to enable others to meet, know, and love him. To do this well, it will take many more authors, many more books, and many more years. This is because "Father Joseph is like a wide-open country whose landmarks we have barely begun to explore: one particular mountain, one particular river, one particular plain." These words come from Eugene Notermans, a Volunteer and companion of Father Joseph for twenty-five years. "As for Father Joseph's life," he adds, "our own existences will not be long enough to take in all the facets of it."

Father Joseph: a country to explore; first and foremost a country to live in. Here is a man whom we all have to rediscover by

---

1 Long-term Volunteers join the International Movement ATD Fourth World by deciding to make an ongoing commitment, dedicating their lives and skills to the cause of the very poor. They often live in the community they serve and choose to receive a minimum salary. Single or married, they live and work in teams.

living with him today and in times to come. For he dared to live with us the future that human beings are dreaming of, even when we were not yet able to fathom it ourselves. He lived the love and hope that the poorest of the poor, more than anyone else, are forced to imagine because their efforts to love and to hope are constantly thwarted. They always sensed at once these feelings Father Joseph was experiencing. From Amsterdam to Manila, from London to Port-au-Prince, from Marseilles to Guatemala City and Ouagadougou, they knew as soon as they laid eyes on him that he was on their side and from their side of the tracks. They knew that he was proposing what they, themselves, longed for, even if they did not dare to admit it to themselves. We have seen the poor amazed, but never really bewildered, by what he was saying and undertaking. Indeed, he was expressing their own hopes, even if this might seem disturbing to them, risky sometimes, and hard to grasp in all its dimensions. Holding your head high, standing up for people even poorer than yourself, believing in your own worth and that of others — where could all of this lead them?

For long-term Volunteers and friends, the questions raised by this man coming from the depths of extreme poverty were just as numerous. Like the Fourth World families, they, too, followed him intuitively and with confidence, before understanding everything. Now, however, we really have to understand in order to continue that to which Father Joseph devoted his life. To accomplish this, we are going to try, not to reminisce about him, but to walk again in his presence with pens in hand. Our goal is to see more clearly together where he continues to lead us, whatever our convictions and beliefs may be. Born into deepest poverty, he was offered the chance to escape from it alone. By refusing to abandon his own, he truly made the poorest of the poor his people. But then, all human beings, rich and poor of all creeds, became equally essential to him. The human race became his dwelling place and the setting for his life and his deeds. He knowingly chose this motto for his priesthood: "Put out into deep water and pay out your nets for a catch." From then on, no human being would leave him untouched.

Charles Ehlinger, the editor of Father Joseph's first book, said of him: "Those who have met him, even if only once, know that it was vital for him to bear witness to the Church of the poor — not to the Church on the one hand and the poor on the other, but to the Church and the poor inseparably, in the same breath." Charles Ehlinger was right, but there is more to it. It has always been essential for Father Joseph to bear witness to the fact that all of humanity is inseparable from its poorest members; that the poor are the Church, because they are humanity.

In 1964 he wrote: "No one, wherever he may come from, is completely intact as long as extreme poverty is mutilating some of his brothers. And every human being, whatever his beliefs, becomes whole when he turns those very poor into the first among his brothers. Everyone knows this in his heart of hearts. And everyone is called on to rid the world of extreme poverty." He not only believed that all people had the same calling to begin the job here and now, but he also was sure that everyone would really go to work if only they met other people ready to take action with them.

Father Joseph believed in all human beings. But he believed first and foremost in the poorest of the poor.

> Hold onto a sense of wonder in spite of it all
> ...
> Because they are human beings.
> Believe that they will be able to cope ...
> Be sure that the miracle will happen,
> that after days of tension, anger, and violence,
> there will follow, closer and closer together,
> days of understanding, exchange, and affection.
> Feel certain about this because they are human beings;
> this is what it means to fight against extreme poverty.
>
> Believe in spite of it all
> that this is true,
> and that they will fulfill their humanity...
> Believe that they will be able to give and receive love,
> even though their hearts have so often been deceived,
> belittled, cast aside, humiliated, and betrayed.
> And even — why not! — be sure that their souls will be able to pray;
> this is what it means to fight against extreme poverty.

To be torn apart by their cuts,
wounded by their wounds,
bloodied by their beatings ...
hoping within their hope,
loving within their love,
praying within their prayer,
in order to face suffering with them,
in order to hunt it down, to annihilate it,
this is what it means to destroy extreme poverty.

Far beyond ideas, intentions, and wishes,
paying the price of freedom and justice,
of rights and of powers,
means bringing into humanity
true charity for all.

These are excerpts from a meditation by Father Joseph in 1969. In this first book, we are setting out anew to discover the man who shared so fully his certainty that the most crushed among families would stand up again. It is essential for these families to get to know him better and better. They are the first heirs, the first ones called on to continue, and the first ones responsible for making him known to others. And what is vital to the families is also vital to the Volunteer Corps and to friends. A mother from a family in extreme poverty in the Netherlands said, "If we do not cherish Father Joseph today, he will die twice. That would be unbearable." "What does cherishing him mean?" we asked her. "Keeping him in our minds, in our hearts, and in our lives, and teaching our children about him."

# Chapter One

# A POOR CHILD HAS NO CHILDHOOD

## Parents Absorbed by a Humiliating Struggle

Born on February 12, 1917, Joseph Wresinski, like many very poor children, never knew exactly where he saw the light of day. This was the time when the Great War of 1914-1918 was totally exhausting the meager supplies of the poor in France. Foreigners in the country, the Wresinski family was experiencing untold hardships. The father, a native of Poznan in Pomerania, a Polish region occupied by Germany at the time of his emigration, was the bearer of a German passport. For the Wresinskis and their first son, this meant confinement in the Fort of Saumur, and later in an abandoned secondary school in Angers, France, when the war with Germany broke out. The mother, of Spanish extraction, gave birth to a little girl who, through lack of medical care, died from bronchopneumonia.

Is this also where Joseph drew his first breath? His parents never made it altogether clear to him. Here, however, is what Sister Antoinette, a religious of the Sisters of the Good Shepherd, later remembers: "Joseph was born in the former secondary school of Angers, not far from Saint-Serge; that was where they used to put refugees." His birth certificate states, with no further details, that he was born on Boreau Street in Angers. Yet, in all likelihood, he saw the light of day in a maternity ward housed under the eaves of the former main secondary school of Angers, next to the place where political internees were sheltered. His parents did not bring the subject up with him more than once, and Father Joseph himself taught us later that men and women in extreme poverty often feel the need to erase from their minds memories that are too painful and humiliating. We do know that having been interned as suspects and having been deprived of all honorable ways to earn a living remained such a memory for the Wresinski parents.

Family memory, however, will retain the fact that there was no doctor during delivery, even though the mother was very weak. Her husband did not move from her bedside. Only two days later, the birth was reported to the city clerk's office. The birth certificate indicates as witnesses two men who were living in a nearby almshouse, both of whom, unskilled and illiterate, were unable to sign the document.

Once the war was over, the family moved into a former blacksmith's shop on Saint-Jacques Street, close to a neighborhood accommodating a large number of very poor households. This workshop and an adjacent building had been more or less transformed into living space. The Wresinski household occupied a part of the ground floor, including a small room facing the street. Wladyslaw Wresinski set up shop there as a watchmaker. His Polish diploma as engineer-mechanic (his family said that he was a sanitary engineer) did not ensure him any comparable employment in France. Without rights or help of any kind, he had to come up with a way of earning a living if the household was not to remain condemned to relying on charity. However, this foray into watchmaking was short-lived. Mr. Wresinski had to close his shop when a thief broke in and stole the only gold watch that had been entrusted to him. His sense of honor was all the more easily hurt since it had been undermined for years and since the suspicion of having been on the enemy's side during the war had followed him into his new neighborhood. This was why he decided to sell the little that he owned, including a few tools, in order to reimburse the owner of the watch. Neither he nor his family recovered from this blow for a long time.

As for Mr. Wresinski himself, he became obsessed with regaining his honor, both as a man and as a worker. This obsession made him violent and, in the long run, he sacrificed his family to it. He had only one idea: leave Angers and start a new life somewhere else. He went looking for employment in other cities, farther and farther away, without much success at first. Afraid that she would not find another roof to put over her children's heads, his wife did not dare to follow him. So this father became an irregular visitor to his household, coming to see them less and less frequently. He would come home whenever some slightly better paying job enabled him to buy his wife and children clothes, food, and toys, and sometimes even a beautiful luxury item like a vase. Then he would leave again. It is to one such unexpected return that we owe the only photograph of the family, all dressed up in new clothes for the occasion.

These were the depression years; we can imagine all the determination this humiliated man needed not to give up his dream. Eventually he did fulfill it, but only by going back to Poland for good. He still managed to send some things to his wife, but at the same time he asked her for a divorce. She refused, in spite of the help she knew she could obtain if she abandoned this husband who was no longer taking care of his family.

*The Wresinski family, circa 1928. Joseph is on the left. "I learned everything from my mother."*

In fact, the mother also clung fiercely to her idea of family honor. Around 1910, she had been a school teacher in Spain; now during this trying period between the two world wars in France, she found only rough housecleaning jobs. She went to work on foot, struggling to climb the steep streets leading to the upper city where well-to-do families lived. She never earned enough to move out of the blacksmith's shop on Saint-Jacques Street or even to satisfy the basic needs of her children, who were four in number in 1923: Louis, Joseph, Antoinette, and Martin.

Mrs. Wresinski experienced her husband's absence as an abandonment. As a foreigner, she could never find it in her heart to take root in a country that had treated her husband as an enemy and had let her baby die in confinement. At the same time, ever since this detention, she lived in fear of being sent back across the border. She had benefactors, but no friends. Single-handedly, she withstood the intrusions of ladies of the parish who, in the name of charity, thought that they should run her life. "Madam, your son would get a much better education in the Auteuil Orphanage." Single-handedly, she also defended her son despite the advice of the parochial school principal: "Madam, you know quite well that your children are unable to learn. It's a waste of time to enroll your son Joseph for the graduation certificate."

With her back to the wall, Mrs. Wresinski refused to put her son in foster care. "My children aren't orphans!" Father Joseph would remember this: "What stores of indignation and bravery my mother needed to stand up for her children this way. This was at a time when Father Brottier was leading a major drive on behalf of this organization in Auteuil, which Saint Theresa of Lisieux had honored in her prayers. For such a poor mother, wasn't refusing to send her son there an insult to Church charities?" Mrs. Wresinski did not let that stop her. One day, defying the school principal's disapproving look, she went to enroll her son for the graduation certificate as an independent student. He obtained it and he would not forget that he owed it to his constantly humiliated mother, who was rarely able to put her affection into words but who, for her children's sake, was able to show all kinds of courage.

Only later would Joseph understand his father, and from then on he would never stop standing up for men who are out of work: "An unemployed man is a humiliated human being. He can't let life humiliate him like this without reacting. And a poor man, now as in the past, is going to react in the same violent way." As a child, Joseph feared his father. Toward his mother, he would feel boundless respect and love. With her, he would learn everything about extreme poverty, but also about the resistance that a mother can put up against it. "Always the target of the mistrust and judgments of people surrounding her, she had to appear more perfect, better educated, more faithful, and more energetic than others in order to find favor, compassion, and support."

## Destitution, Shame, and Violence

Life is too hard for Mrs. Wresinski to be able to think about bringing her children up on hugs and kisses. Misery has prevented her from being just another mother. Survival and family unity are so fragile that she has to call on her children to help provide for the most basic needs. She puts them to work. Joseph, at age four, is in the street before six o'clock in the morning, winter and summer alike. He goes to earn his breakfast plus two francs a week as an altar boy at the second mass with the Sisters of the Good Shepherd. "My mother must have felt our hunger very keenly to have consented to put me out into the street like this every day, when I was so little. I must also have been aware of her anguish to have accepted this constraint without letting it embitter my heart or make me insult God. In all kinds of weather, head bowed and back bent, steeped in sleep, but also screaming with anger sometimes, I would walk along the Rue Saint-Jacques, follow the Rue Brault, empty and forbidding, down to the meadows, and then serve mass with the Sisters so that forty cents would be given to my mother."

Later, as a child, he will hold many other odd jobs. Father Joseph knows what he's talking about when he says, in 1983, "Today, as in the past, poor children have no childhood; responsibilities overtake them as soon as they can stand up." He runs errands himself for the nearby butcher's wife, then spends endless evenings fitting together Zig-Zag cigarette papers. "This was subcontracting work. Every evening, and on Saturdays and Sundays, we used to insert sheaves of Zig-Zag cigarette papers into cardboard holders. We used to bring our boxes to the factory on Montesquieu Street every Thursday to get a little money." Besides, he has to return each day to the convent door to receive a metal container of split peas or lentils for the family table. His older brother, Louis, remembers this too. "It was in used five-liter jelly cans. We got this food from the Madeleine Sisters, penitents who made do with next to nothing themselves." We shouldn't forget the road Joseph traveled as a boy to the gas works either, where he sorted out on the slag heap enough chips of coal to light up their broken-down stove. The children learned to stop up the cracks in the stove with clay they found in the neighboring meadows. "Paths of shame...

This is how destitution, shame, and violence were linked from childhood on."

To be sure, Joseph very quickly becomes an unruly child who talks with his fists. In their lodgings there is no way to let off steam. His only thought is to join his playmates outside in running around, in catching up with life, though he is the target of neighborhood teasing because he is bowlegged as the result of a poorly treated case of rickets. Sister Antoinette of the Good Shepherd Order remembers that he also went to the children's club of the Church. "Still, he must not have stayed there for long; he was such a terror. As soon as he got to the chapel, he used to pray with his hands squeezed together under his chin. He was very devout. A priest, Father Coiscault, used to say that there was certainly something special about this child. Other people were much more reluctant; he was so terrible!"

Father Joseph will explain to us much later: "Violence became for me, as it had for my father, a way to free myself from the countless humiliations that our extreme poverty made us endure." Until the end of his life, he will share the suffering of children in utter poverty with running noses, hoarse voices, and twisted bodies, whose hearts are humiliated and whose movements are violent.

However, by sharing adults' troubles too soon, Joseph develops an unusual sensitivity to his mother's sufferings. He finds her at night, sitting in her unheated kitchen, praying. "It was almost always cold in our home. One of our walls was made of crates covered with wrapping paper. When the paper split, cold drafts lashed out at us. My mother used to remain motionless on her chair, asking the Lord for solutions that surely would have to be credited to a miracle, given the poverty we were living in. Maybe she was also simply asking Him to help her endure problems that had no solution, to know how to get along with them, keeping in mind — as she used to say to her children — that there were always people even poorer than us."

Father Joseph's later understanding of what families in grinding poverty around the world go through and hope for will not be derived merely from intuition. It comes to him from the everyday experience of his childhood. It comes to him from this mother of his, constantly hard pressed, who by day only knows how to talk about money and, at night, talks to God. The very poor families whom he will meet in every country will make no mistake about it. Father Joseph does not only share their sorrows in the name of a solidarity he has chosen; he has kept within himself the vulnerability of all those who have experienced extreme poverty since childhood. "Anyone born into extreme poverty will always remain a poor person." The men, women, and children to whom he will be committed as an adult and a priest, will always find in him more than just tenderness. They will recognize the brotherhood and the complicity of someone who has been through it all himself.

## Chapter Two

# ADOLESCENCE: A PREPARATION FOR WHAT STRUGGLE?

### Joseph, an Apprentice Pastry Cook

In 1930, after making sure her son got his elementary school graduation certificate, Mrs. Wresinski accomplished another feat. At a time when underemployment was prevalent among young people from the neediest backgrounds, she obtained for her son a position as an apprentice helper in a bakery shop. He had noticed the sign himself, displayed in a nearby bakery. It was his mother who wrenched from the owner the promise to take her boy whose rough behavior was known throughout the whole neighborhood.

So, at age thirteen, Joseph was no longer wholly dependent on his mother. His older brother was seventeen and had begun to earn his living as a wood sculptor. This was still not enough to break the hold of poverty on his mother, who had her two other children still in school. However, life was becoming somewhat less difficult; things were brightening up; there seemed to be a future in sight. But what lingers the most in the memory of Joseph's brothers, whom we can still question, are those years of sheer misery. They seem to have filled up all the space, as they did in the memory of Father Joseph himself. "Surely, however, like poor children today, I used to play and laugh. Surely, I used to create my own secret corners, my hiding places, and my exploratory routes in downtown Angers where I used to make up labyrinths with my friends. But there was this road to and from the convent that I had to follow every day — the path of shame of my childhood, which has wiped from my memory anything that might have been a consolation."

Father Joseph did keep other memories from this period of his adolescence, when he had begun to discover what would gradually become the purpose of his lifetime struggle. However, he was going to become a man who did not talk much about himself. He would speak about his childhood, especially to tell about the terrible poverty in those days, his mother's hardships, and what they taught him. Apart from that, he would talk about the extreme poverty of Fourth World families, about their struggle and the Movement he founded with them, and, obviously, about the Church and the Gospel. He would hardly ever talk about himself again.

Charles Ehlinger observed, not without some surprise: "It did not take anyone long to notice that Father Joseph never indulged in talking about himself. He was not in the habit of telling his own story. Modesty carried to this extreme is something very rare and surprising in texts where biography and autobiography play such a great role." Those who were his constant companions know that his own person mattered little to him. His unpretentiousness was not a character trait that he had chosen and developed; it was an integral part of him. He was discreet and shy, not like people who are afraid of getting into trouble, but like people who feel that they, themselves, are not the real issue. Was this why he forgave and forgot all offenses so quickly? His shyness disappeared as soon as he had to talk about the poorest of the poor or about God. As for his humility, it was inseparable from his very being. Let us see what else we can learn from him about his young years before the seminary.

Concerning his apprenticeship in Angers, in Saumur, and then in Nantes, we know that the harsh conditions of this era did not frighten him. "Conditions," he used to say, "begin to become a burden to you when you cannot feel proud of your profession." Did he think he had found his calling? Curious by nature, he loved to learn. And "pastry-making is an artistic profession, after all. The act of kneading, of taking dough and shaping it as you wish, to ensure the finishing touch that will make it perfect... The Convent of the Good Shepherd and my profession as pastry cook taught me about architecture, about the sense of proportion, about the grace of curves. This is why I have never stopped building." According to his older brother, a real craftsman himself, he did not, however, consider the pastry-making trade a lifetime calling. He enjoyed exploring the world, had other interests. Among these were his former companions, less fortunate than himself, who, in the best of cases, found employment in factories, as unskilled workmen, particularly with the paint manufacturer Valentine.

*Rue Saint-Jacques in Angers.*
*"The sun never got inside."*

In fact, Joseph grew up in a working-class area bordering on an extremely poor neighborhood. He lived in a refurbished blacksmith's shop, which stuck out on Saint-Jacques Street. It would have appeared less out of place in the nearby Saint-Nicolas neighborhood. There was a lot of dilapidated housing there, where families hard hit by unending deprivations were crowded together. In short, Joseph grew up on the borderline between a plain working-class environment and an area characterized by overwhelming poverty. He lived in the former setting but, unlike many others, had friends in the latter. For reasons he would not explain, he kept in touch with them even when his path in life had already led him elsewhere. Can an event from his childhood perhaps give us a clearer picture?

"One day, one of the oldest boys in school became furious with a boy weaker than himself. He cornered him against the foot of the toilet wall and punched and kicked him. What happened inside me? I threw myself at him. Now it was my turn to kick and punch him. I scratched his face until the teacher came to drag me away by force.

"Why had I done this? This puny little boy was nothing to me. What was I doing defending him? It was he, however, who remained in my memory and not the punishment I brought upon myself. I was expelled from school, but I hardly remember anything that happened after the fight. What does stay in my mind as a turning point was this boy getting himself beaten up by someone so much stronger than he was. Today, it seems that this was the starting point of a fight in which I would probably be the loser but which, due to my obstinacy, I would carry on for the rest of my life."

## First Steps in the World of Trade Unions

Indeed, all first-hand accounts of his adolescence talk about the ardor with which Joseph defends other youths who apparently mean nothing to him. He has not lost his fiery intensity. Why is he making this kind of personal investment? Why do we find this future craftsman debating issues in the midst of unqualified workers from the Valentine paint factory? Why, at age sixteen, does he keep company with members of the Communist Youth groups? This is not really where he belongs, people from his former neighborhood think. From his meetings with the Communist Youth groups, he will retain gratitude and knowledge that he will never disown. Above all, he learns that being an activist requires training. He does not remain with the Communist Youth groups for long. Still, he will always acknowledge a strong feeling of friendship for those grass-roots activists, both youths and adults, who really commit themselves to changing their comrades' destinies, wearing themselves out with field work and putting themselves through training sessions that take their entire vacations.

One evening in 1934 in Nantes, a friend invited him to go to a meeting of the Young Christian Workers' Association (*Jeunesse Ouvrière Chrétienne*). He was seventeen and he would remember this all his life. In fact, that evening, though merely an unknown guest, he would be entrusted by the chaplain with writing the summary of the meeting. He had never handled anything like this and yet other people were ready to trust him! On his hospital bed, forty-five years later, he would repeat the conviction instilled in him then. This was the answer he would give to a Fourth World Volunteer who told him about his fear of lacking skills: "But who do you think is competent? No one is ever competent in matters of poverty and justice. We become competent by accepting the tasks that are given to us. The Young Christian Workers taught me that when I was seventeen."

Joseph stayed with the Young Christian Workers until he left for the seminary in 1936. After being ordained a priest, he would support this organization in his parishes. For the time being, he was learning from it, as he had from the Communist Youth groups, a discipline that would be useful to him over the years to come. He helped conduct surveys which, by their thoroughness, represented one of the strong points of Young Christian Workers. "From them, I learned not only how to observe, but also how to make notes in order to understand things better." This is what he would say to us Volunteers quite a while later in the emergency housing camp of Noisy-le-Grand,[2] when all of us would be amazed to find him with a pencil always at hand. In the evening, he filled the pages of a thick gray accounting book with notes. He used to record facts from the daily lives of the poorest families of these times. Soon he would suggest that members of the Volunteer Corps beginning to take shape around him write daily observation reports. In the long run, these reports would turn the Volunteer Corps into the chronicler of the poorest of our time. With Father Joseph, the Volunteer Corps would write thirty years of their history around the world, thirty years of their memory of the past too, which Father Joseph would teach Volunteers to scrutinize. Ultimately, the pencil that was at the start of this whole endeavor was inherited by the Volunteer Corps, through Father Joseph, from the Young Christian Workers.

The period of the Young Christian Workers was also the time when Joseph, who often returned to Saint-Jacques Street, began to pray again. He found his way back to the parish church of his childhood and met with the Sisters of the Good Shepherd again. One of them had spoken to Joseph in 1921, when he was the little boy of four whom she saw every day trotting down Brault Street beside a goat that his mother sent him to put out to graze in low-lying meadows. "What would you think about coming to mass each morning

2 Noisy-le-Grand is the name of the town where the emergency housing camp was constructed in 1954 on a former rubbish dump on the edge of marshlands. Some 300 families lived there in fibrocement huts known as "igloos", without electricity and with only five water pumps to serve 2,000 people. Birthplace of the International Movement ATD Fourth World, the emergency housing camp was finally replaced in 1970, thanks to Father Joseph's efforts, by a Housing Program for the Social Advancement of the Family.

as an altar boy?" the Sister asked Joseph. "I'll give your mother forty cents each week." "These two francs persuaded me," Father Joseph would say. "At home, my parents only talked about money."

In 1936, when Joseph was a young man of nineteen, another Sister of the convent turned to him again. "What would you think if someone paid for your studies in the seminary?" Once again, the question was put in terms of money. However, Joseph no longer saw it in the same way. Financial security was no longer at stake since he now was an assistant pastry cook. He had already worked as a substitute in various small market towns. He could get along from now on and even keep the wolf away from his mother's door. What could studying and going back to school to learn Latin at nineteen lead to? This time, the offer of money seemed liable to jeopardize a secure future. Furthermore, was Joseph not better suited for the trade unions' struggle? Why did he choose to go to the seminary? Here is how he would answer this question fifty years later.

"Through the Young Christian Workers' struggle, I began to think about freeing my brothers. And fighting for them, fighting so that no other family would ever have to be like mine, meant becoming a priest of Jesus Christ, crucified and risen. You can't imagine how wonderful these times were. I now knew for a fact that my life fit into an eternal plan, that the poor would hear the good news, and that I would contribute to changing men's hearts. In fact, for me, everything was linked. Having regained my faith not only meant finding the reason for struggling — I had it already — it meant devoting my life to Jesus Christ."

# Chapter Three

# "A CHOICE THAT NO ONE COULD HAVE IMAGINED"

## The Education of a Heart Overwhelmed by Injustice

Father Joseph's calling will remain a secret between himself and God. This vocation amazes each of us all the more since we shall never be able to understand it in the light of all that he himself taught us about deepest poverty. Such deprivation thwarts all attempts at loving. How did Father Joseph learn to love God while growing up with parents who shouted out their suffering during quarrels? What resources could Mrs. Wresinski count on to educate her children's hearts?

"Extreme poverty suffocates love. Husband and wife, parents and children, lack the means to do things that tell someone else: I love you. Love withers when you can do nothing to express it." Father Joseph was speaking from experience. He never stopped pointing out to families, whose life he shared in the emergency housing camp of Noisy-le-Grand, the smallest action that anyone took to make family and friends less miserable:

"As for Jean-Christophe, things are going to be all right since you're trying so hard to send him to school."

"Your wife is lucky she's got you. The way you're filling up the cracks, the baby will be warm."

"Your father is very brave to go out looking for scrap metal in weather like this...."

He would often remind the Church how urgent it is to record with loving care each gesture of the poorest that evokes God. "We should never stop emphasizing all the help and tenderness they offer one another. We should never stop discovering these humble actions, sources of grace."

While he was preparing for a television show in 1981, here is what he told us Volunteers: "We have to know what we want to get across." And he gave this example: "I remember the time when people came to our home to wrench from my mother the piano that she had inherited from an aunt. It had come from Spain and my mother had her heart set on keeping it. Maybe one of her children would like music and the piano would help that one get off to a good start. So the piano sat there, its feet sinking into the worm-eaten floor. Then came the day when people began to say, 'If these folks have a piano, then they have money, and it's not worth the trouble to give them any assistance.' That was how my mother was forced to sell the piano for an absurdly low price. In exchange for help, she had to sell hope. This piano enabled her to cherish an illusion about my little sister's future. It was a way to love her children and to show them her love, which people were tearing away from her in the name of helping the poor. If we succeed in showing this type of reality on television, we shall be getting across what it means to be poor.

"Extreme poverty separates people from things that are vital to them because they provide their hands, their eyes, their tongues, and their hearts with habits — habits that open them up to a culture of the hands, the heart, and the mind and that enable them to build relations with others. Such constant, intense deprivation prevents people in the long run from thinking like everyone else. Even their spiritual life is affected by it."

Was this not what happened to Mrs. Wresinski, a woman of faith and culture who, having been haunted for too long by a lack of money, could talk about nothing else to her children? She continued, nevertheless, to practice acts of mercy. She used to invite to her table the son of a lady next door who had taken to drink and was not preparing meals any longer. She used to give bread to other people when she was running out of it herself. Still, as Father Joseph used to explain: "Extreme poverty poisons even these acts of mercy. In the end, people are always getting into arguments and then they will say, 'After all I have done for them...' Besides, those who hand out assistance never miss an opportunity to point out:

'Ma'am, I'm giving this to you for your children.' 'Here, I'm giving you some candy; be sure to keep it for yourself.' Those who give to the poor have a hard time letting go of their possession. They go on watching over it, monitoring the recipient. 'Is he going to use it wisely; isn't he going to sell it or waste it?' Would my mother really make me wear shoes that had been given to her and that, by the way, were not even my size? That's how my poor mother was forced to lie. 'Of course, Ma'am, my son is happy with his ankle-boots, and you can just imagine how my children ate up all the bread!' This is how people in poverty are split apart, cut off from those who give to them, but also divided among themselves, unaccustomed to sharing openly, giving stealthily only to regret it a moment later. Neighbors become people to avoid because their misfortune is so obvious, but helping them will get us into trouble with the social worker. This causes muted hatred where peace and solidarity should prevail."

We do not know how young Joseph's heart became the heart of a priest of Jesus Christ in spite of this existence, where everything conspired to turn him into a solitary, bitter man trying to make it on his own. How was violence made to serve love? "When I was twelve or thirteen, like all poor children, I began to give everything away — not out of a sense of charity but as a kind of reaction against the obligation of always having to receive. I used to give away everything. My older brother did likewise. We could no longer stand not having the right to give. This lasted until I was eighteen or nineteen years old." In fact, this lasted all his life. It was almost impossible to offer Father Joseph a gift that he would not pass on to others. He never kept anything for himself; his hands did nothing else but pass around, relay, share, and give. Was he perhaps no longer doing it for the same reasons as during his youth? In that case, what happened? How did he become what extreme poverty could not make of him?

What Father Joseph would tell us about it himself leaves the mystery unsolved. He would speak about his mother, who loved him and who knew him well. "She knew that I was not stupid but that I carried too many responsibilities on my shoulders, that I suffered too much, and that I had too deep a perception of injustice. For those of us who received charity, but never what was rightly due to us, injustice was our daily fate. My mother did not want one more injustice to be inflicted on me. It was she who enrolled me for the graduation certificate."

Years later, Father Joseph was still able to identify all those whose love he acknowledged. "During my childhood, I knew a man who honored my mother. He was the parish priest. He used to come to our home to ask for the church offering. He would accept with great dignity the fifty cents that my mother had set aside. He would sit down at the table where we children were packaging Zig-Zag cigarette papers. We would offer him a small pack of them by cheating on the number of sheaves in the other packs, and he would thank us ceremoniously. He used to ask my mother to be of assistance, to make a gesture toward our atheistic neighbors on the upper floor. He respected her. He experienced the honor of sharing and the opportunity to partake of pride and trust with us."

Still, could having known a parish priest and several other people of that caliber have been enough to open up the heart of a child whose entire life was steeped in dishonor? In the first place, how could this child whose heart was overwhelmed by humiliation, know how to recognize and trust those few persons who respected his family? How did his heart learn to believe in human beings' goodness and in God's mercy? Only other children and other adults in grinding poverty can conceive the answers. As for us, we can only surrender before the love and faith that grew in him, against all rhyme and reason. The love of a vulnerable and humble Church — does not part of the mystery, perhaps, lie right there, in that very frailty and humility?

"The Church will always be mocked and cast aside by the world. I discovered this when I was only a lad brought up by my mother, the poorest woman in the Saint-Jacques neighborhood of Angers. I learned to love the Church because my mother was a woman of prayer. Every morning she sent me to the Good Shepherd Convent. I was an altar boy there from the age of four and a half. I loved the beauty of the Church and the serenity of the nuns. Despite that, even as a child, I had a premonition of the fragility of this community and its separation from the neighborhood. I used to say to myself: They have already been driven away in the past; it can still happen to them now. Remember that in those days many did not hide their hostility toward the Church. Also, the fact that one always saw the same people at church, the very small number of men who attended, and the fact that the principal of the so-called public school went to another parish so as not to lose his reputation — all that made me think a lot. In the street, everywhere, posters poked fun at monks and nuns. Sometimes, in shops, people laughed at 'blessed churchoholics'. There was a large gap between the neighborhood and the church in its midst. Of course, the priest was greeted in the street, but I did not feel it was at all sincere. I said to myself, 'The Church means nothing to all of these people.'

"As I grew up, this frailty became even more obvious to me. The Church was so criticized and put down. I saw priests and nuns who were the targets of ridicule and who were even jeered at in the street sometimes. At the time of Vatican II, when I again heard the Church being accused of being pretentious, of possessing money and power, I knew it was not true. I myself had been snubbed, my very cassock insulted too many times to delude myself about the power of the Church. If Christians showed they had any memory, they would know that the Church, like Jesus and the poor, is at the mercy of all the financial, political, and ideological powers."

## Loving a Wretched Jesus

"The Church, like Jesus and the poor ..." In short, God, Jesus, and the Church showed themselves to this young man in the humiliated faces of the destitute, whom the poor themselves find as hard to really respect as do the rich. He loved a vulnerable God, a God handed over to His children. His heart went out to a God about whom he would say later that He is indeed the first one whose rights are scorned. And he loved Jesus who, at the hour of the Temptation in the desert, chose to be the Son of that God up to the very end.

"The hour of the Temptation was not only the moment in which to choose the situation He would embrace in the world; it was the hour in which Jesus deliberately chose the men and women who had to bear that situation. Among the crowd of the poor, Jesus' preference would go to those whom no one but He would choose: the crippled, the lepers, the men of ill repute, the prostitutes, the lame, all those whom the poor themselves tend to ignore and who therefore are the most wretched and vulnerable."

"But how can we lift our eyes on Christ who freely makes this choice and not feel bewildered? Even the very poor themselves would have been unable to make such a choice. As for me, I have been marked and my faith in Jesus' divinity has been sealed, not so much by His miracles or His doctrine, as by the fact that He dared what no other would dare ever before or ever after. He went beyond that freely chosen poverty, which remains a privilege, to identify Himself fully with those who were then and are now at the bottom of the social scale: the outcast lepers, the irremediably disabled, the forsaken paralytics, the possessed and those held to be possessed and therefore banned to living in caves, the spurned prostitutes — in a word, all those who were then and are now held to be marginal."

Marginal — as was the lady next door who had taken to drink; the puny boy who got himself beaten up by someone "so much bigger"; the fellow workers from the Saint-Nicolas district who found no employment. Because he stood up for the puny child who was nothing to him, Joseph was expelled from school. It was so that he could stand up for a wretched Jesus that he was going to follow the path to priesthood. For he was going to do more than just serve Jesus Christ, God, and the Church. He was going to put all his fierce energy into standing up for them. The Church would not be for him just a pretext for serving the poorest. "The poor ***are*** the Church;" God's rights and human rights are inseparable.

Here is how Father Joseph would end the Lord's Prayer one day in 1986, in the midst of Fourth World families:

> Amen, Lord, listen to me.
> May my prayer come true in my life
> because you have been present inside me,
> and because you have forced my hand a little.
>
> You have been so present inside me,
> that I could no longer see anything else
> but you.

Was this not an echo from those distant years of his youth, about which he would say one day: "It was while I was fighting on the side of the poorest and choosing to see things primarily from their point of view that one day I discovered I belonged to the Church, so strongly to the Church that I felt I had to become a priest."

Did his mother, who had understood him so well during his childhood, have a premonition about his calling? In any case, it seems certain that Sister Leroux's idea that her parents could pay for Joseph's studies came from his mother. The two women knew one another and, over the years, Mrs. Wresinski had commanded the nuns' respect. The Leroux parents, farmers in the Tardenois region, regretted not having had a son who could have become a priest. They were quite ready to become sponsors. Still, who but his own mother would have dreamed of proposing this feisty young man? She never breathed a word about it herself nor did Father Douillard, the parish priest, who must have been in on the secret. When Joseph announced to his mother that he wanted to go to the seminary, she just sighed: "At least now I know that you'll be eating every day." A point on which his mother, for once, was wrong about her son Joseph.

# Chapter Four

# SOLDIER, SEMINARIAN, AND BROTHER

## A Seminarian in his Country's Service

In 1936, the decision was finally made. On the advice of Father Douillard, who later became his bishop, Joseph was enrolled in the seminary. Some extra courses were necessary, however, and we shall soon find this nineteen-year-old member of the Young Christian Workers' Association, along with other late starters in discovering a calling, among twelve-year-olds in the secondary school at Beaupréau. Later on, Joseph would also stay for a short while in a school of Latin, run by an elderly priest in the south of France. "It seems to me that I was mainly keeping an eye on my classmates; they were so much younger than I." What humility and what willpower would Joseph need finally to become, when all is said and done, a full-fledged student in a seminary! What perseverance he would need to face the coming years. They would not be quiet or trouble-free ones.

As a matter of fact, on October 15, 1937, the seminarian Joseph Wresinski was inducted into the army. On the 20th, he joined his outfit. We lose sight of him then, only to find him again on October 1, 1938, as a corporal in the 94th Infantry Regiment. On that same day, as supervisor of the barrack-room, he greeted the seminarian Léon Bach, who was also a corporal. This would be the beginning of a lifetime friendship. Thanks to his friend Bach, we now know that, during this period, Joseph met inspection both as a seminarian and as a soldier.

"This was in Bar-le-Duc. He was happy not to be alone any longer as a seminarian surrounded by the wild life of the barracks. At this time, he was already very busy, and he was known in the city. He directed the Community Center for Catholic Soldiers. He organized meetings of the Catholic Action group; he took soldiers to church. He pointed out to them 'places to avoid in the city', and he led tours so that they did actually avoid them. We were two seminarians, and people around us were hostile to us. Still, no one dared to attack us too openly, because, of course, we stood up for each other. Once, they made him do eight days of 'guard duty' because of an argument with a lieutenant who wanted to replace Sunday mass with drilling time. Joseph said no, and he got eight days. I was on guard duty; I was a sergeant then. My friend Joseph came in with his blanket, grumbling about those 'birdbrains'. I sent him back to his barrack-room every evening. We were allies for a long time; there were never any conflicts."

On the front, in 1939, Joseph lived in the trenches. He led patrols even while he suffered from this particularly cold winter. He was promoted to the rank of corporal, first-class. Father Bach tells us, "Joseph was in the front line from the first to the last day. For Christmas 1939, we were on the front in the three frontier areas of Germany, France, and Luxembourg, near Sierck, a village of the Remeling region. For three weeks, it was 27 degrees below Celsius. We were in the forest, facing the Germans. Our bread was frozen, and people were digging holes in the ground to protect themselves against the wind. Joseph had trouble putting up with the cold weather. This may explain the health problems he had later on. In May 1940, the entire 94th Infantry Regiment got orders to leave and was transported to the Department of the Aisne. It was here, near Berry-au-Bac, that Joseph became famous."

Indeed, Corporal, First-Class, Wresinski had spotted French soldiers surrounded by the advancing Germans, on the other side of the Aisne River. He wanted to go fetch them, got into an argument with his lieutenant, and decided to go on his own initiative. That evening, he put together a makeshift raft with his men and crossed the river. On reaching the opposite shore, he tied his raft too loosely and it was carried away by the current. That was when onlookers discovered that Corporal, First-Class, Wresinski did not know how to swim. His men alerted the Special Rescue Squad. The seminarian Bach, who was a member of it, jumped into the water in order to bring him back with a rope.

"Joseph wasn't scared," said Léon Bach, who did not seem to be easily scared himself. "It all ended at Verberie in the Oise. He was again on the front line, while I was defending our Command Headquarters. This adventure lasted a day and a half. On the morning of the first day, the Germans attacked. But a volunteer went to blow up the bridge. It was Joseph. The next day, I heard him at the other end of the village, firing his last bullets to protect escapees, in the midst of widespread cowardice. The junior officers had fled. 'We only had a seminarian to defend us,' his men said. That was when he was taken prisoner. He had fired every shot; he had no ammunition left. Still, he was alive; that was the main thing. The Germans put him with a column of prisoners who were heading toward the north of France. However, Joseph slipped out of the ranks. That was to be expected. You can't keep a character like that in a prisoner-of-war camp; no way!"

Joseph Wresinski's discharge papers state, in fact, that he was taken prisoner on June 11, 1940, at Verberie. He was detained in Frontstalag 101 in Valenciennes, until July 11. The discharge papers do not mention what another prisoner remembers, namely that "if we ate, it was really because of him. He forced the Germans to let us go out looking for food supplies. He was the one who went, anyway." In any event, on July 25, Corporal, First-Class, Wresinski escaped. The seminarian returned to his seminary on foot.

## Looking for the Poor

The man whom he would call "my pal Bach" all his life was going to see him again in 1942. Joseph paid him a visit then in the Seminary for Overseas Missionaries. "He was enthusiastic; he was dreaming about doing things." Joseph was dreaming about them and was doing them too. In Soissons, he spent all his spare time in housing developments where the most deprived families of town were put up (for example, the emergency housing projects of Saint-Crépin, Saint-Médard, and others). He also organized children's summer camps. Then, since the seminary was transferred to the monastery of Entrammes in the Mayenne region, he would spend his vacations where he had lived as a youth.

Father Pardon, another seminary companion, addressed these lines to Father Joseph in his parish newsletter the day after Father Joseph was called back to his Lord: "Joseph — I never called you anything but 'Joseph' since the days when we were next-door neighbors in the monastery of Entrammes. We even used to give you a simpler name, 'the Brother', because you always had that word on the tip of your tongue. You consorted with princes and powerful people, but you conscientiously remained the outsider, the man of poverty, the man of misery. I remember your vacations as a seminarian, which you spent in the Valentine paint factory as a manual laborer doing heavy work. I can still see you, after you returned from those exhausting days, dozing peacefully during the courses about dogma or Holy Scripture to make up for lost sleep."

We also encounter the man whom his co-seminarians called "the Brother" in a mine in De Sessevalle, near Douai, once again during vacation time. He came to see his friend, the future Father François Sans, and asked him to arrange for him to go down into a mine. "He wanted to get to know about their life and, for more than a month, he went to work at the bottom. It was a very deep pit; and, with a pick and a pickaxe, he went to find out about cutting and hewing. This was very hard work, especially for him since he was not used to it. This was even truer since he did not stop there. As soon as he came to the top, he went to visit the families of those with whom he was working. He really wanted to share their lives. He didn't have his own room; he shared one with children, who were three or four." This is how Father Sans' sister recounts her memories. She adds, "My brother told him, 'You're going to kill yourself.' In fact, he did catch a terrible case of dysentery. He really wanted to 'be with' people and not just to 'see' them. He should have been more careful. After spending eight hours at the bottom of the pit, he would ride a bike to go see the families, play with the children, take an interest in the lives of miners' wives. He wanted to know everything; I can remember this as if it was yesterday. He did not get any sleep."

Was not sleeping during vacations but dozing during Holy Scripture courses a good way to study? His passion, the Old Testament,

*Joseph, a seminarian, at the De Sessevalle mine.*

does not seem to have suffered too much from this. As a parish priest in Dhuizel, he astonished his colleagues in the diocese. "Joseph is among those who take charge of catechism. The Dominicans who come each month to Braine, especially Father Féret, put fresh life into our understanding of the Old Testament. To our surprise, Joseph possesses a vast biblical learning! He doesn't hesitate to quote prophets like Amos and Ezekiel. Not only does he recite passages, but he also gives the references by heart."

The seminarians of Entrammes readily agree that "he studies eagerly." But they also witness his eagerness to go back to the poor (he will spend time repeatedly in the Mission de France[3]). Above all, it is the slightly marginal brother who stays in their memories. All the more so since each time he comes back from vacation, he writes for hours in his room in the middle of the night. They do not quite realize that he is a former member of the Young Christian Workers, recording his observations about factories, mines, and men who have trouble breathing because they are grinding powder all day long in a cistern tank in the poorly ventilated basement of a paint factory. He writes everything down "so that nothing of the life of the poor will be lost," as he will tell us himself, twenty years later.

3 Mission de France is a Catholic training and resource center open to priests and religious to prepare them for the evangelization and pastoral care of the poor.

Father Babilotte from the monastery of Solignac recalls this seminarian who was not altogether like the others. "He was in a theology class and I was in a preparatory course for late starters. I had very little contact with him ... Even so, I did have time to recognize in him someone who distinguished himself by his iron will to do something out of the ordinary. He was truly a headstrong, bold, dynamic, and fiery man, a man of the Gospel who wanted to bring the Good News to the poor and to the poorest of the poor. When he spoke about his upcoming apostolate, it was always in terms of seeking out the masses."

The seminarians of those days also remember a Joseph who, during those years of occupation and of scarcity, went out to find food supplies. He was by far the most experienced in this matter, and his superiors let him do things his way, "as long as people did not notice it too much." "The poorest one of us all saw to it that we got enough to eat."

However, what do we know about Father Joseph's own memories? We have mentioned that he did not talk much about himself. Still, he would confide to us how grateful he remained throughout his priesthood to have had Jesuits as professors, how he began to quench his thirst for reading and learning. "From a very early age, I refused to be condemned to ignorance. My mother had refused this for me. But it was only in the seminary that I could begin to make up for lost time. In the seminary, I began to quench the thirst for reading I felt since my childhood; I read everything that I could lay my hands on. This was when I began to read and reread Saint Augustine for months on end." He would also tell us how, during those years, he was affected by some of his elders like Father Godin and Father Depierre. "I feasted on these priests who became oppressed peoples' witnesses and advocates." Father Depierre, who had already immersed himself in a working-class parish, wrote to him:

> The priesthood, you see, it has only been for barely two years that I have understood what it means. It's something big... Staying up until two o'clock in the morning, wearing yourself out, and falling down from exhaustion, this is nothing at all; it just has to be done. But the essential part of it is being another Christ, being a saint. For, you see, these people

> are consumers. That's what is wonderful, and, if the priest doesn't answer their expectations, they look at him, sad and astonished. Then feeling disgusted, they leave him and they are lost to the working class... Therefore, don't waste a minute in the seminary; fill yourself full of Jesus. Rethink all your dogma; live ethics in terms of reality. You feel crushed, so do I... I swear to you that I have never regretted being a priest.

Father Joseph was to go farther, beyond the working class to the very heart of extreme poverty, which no combat had reached as yet. Still, he would always feel a strong friendship for such priests as Father Depierre who inspired him during his years in the seminary.

## Chapter Five

# "WE WERE LIVING IN THE HOPE OF REALLY BECOMING THE POOR"

### The First Parish: "To Plunge Even Deeper into Suffering Mankind."

"Jesus Christ made me a priest on June 29, 1946, in the Cathedral of Soissons."

The souvenir picture of Father Joseph's ordination shows Jesus facing an urban neighborhood that is receding into the night. In the foreground, there are workers' dwellings with lighted windows. In the background, factory smokestacks are still spewing forth their smoke into a darkened sky. Above this, are these words: "I take pity on this crowd."

At the moment of his ordination, as we can see, Father Joseph was a young French priest in step with his time. In the seminary, besides the activities that his co-seminarians remembered, he spent countless hours reading. He became extremely well versed in the history of the French Catholic Church for the period between the two World Wars and the years of the Occupation. During our later talks about those days, he mentioned all the famous authors of this era and we would find signs of them in the modest library that he had carried with him in a crate from parish to parish. All those who knew him as a young priest, ("Father Joseph," they called him, "our parish priest," and so on) recalled that he used to read a lot. "In the rectory in Tergnier, he had only one room. That was where he slept and held his meetings with young people. There was no heating, but the mantelpiece was covered with books." "In the rectory of Dhuizel there was only one room fit to live in, and it was filled with books." "In his shack in the emergency housing camp of Noisy-le-Grand, he had nothing, only a bed, just a mattress in fact, and books were piled up on the ground."

Which books are we talking about? There was Saint Augustine, of course — part of the *Confessions*, of *Sermons on the Psalms*, and *The Christian Doctrine* ("I never had the means to collect all the standard works of the man who was the first of my masters") — followed closely by works of Bernanos, Malraux, LeRoy, Claudel, Saint-Exupéry, Teilhard de Chardin, Emmanuel Mounier, Maritain, Chenu, Giraudoux, Daniel-Rops, as well as Zola, Thorez, and Lenin. There were also works by Lhande, Daniel and Godin. Then came Canon Boulard, Father Voillaume, Van der Meersch, Fathers Lagrange, Lebreton, and Prat (all the *Lives of Jesus*). "Everyone was reading them," Father Joseph explained twenty years later when we were putting his library in order. "I didn't have the means to collect books, but these ones were easy to get." Congar and Lubac stood beside old issues of the magazine *Esprit*, the "*Cahiers des Semaines Sociales*," and encyclical letters of Leo XIII, Pius X, Pius XI, and others. There were also several authors that perhaps not everyone was reading, such as Gorky, Dostoyevski, and Tolstoy, who were later joined by all the great Russian dissidents. Many volumes were second-hand and bore marks of previous owners.

On the whole, these readings were certainly in tune with the times. Would the slightly marginal seminarian fit into the lifestyle of young priests of his time after all? "I take pity on this crowd," certainly was the language of an entire Church that had discovered a dechristianized urban and a rural France. Here was a country composed of clearly divided urban and rural masses, separated from the more prosperous classes; each one of them was leading its own life. The Church had understood that, to find its way back to these masses, it must embrace the everyday facts of their lives as well as their way of thinking and speaking.

Out of this discovery, the Young Christian Workers' Association was born in the 1920s. This same discovery would spark the creation of the Mission de France, the Frères Missionaires des

Campagnes, the Little Brothers of Father de Foucauld, and the teams of Robert Garric, for example. A wide range of religious, social, cultural, trade-union, and even political initiatives provided priests with numerous opportunities to plunge deeply into the everyday realities of the lives of people — especially of the poor. How could Father Joseph's calling to a wretched Jesus Christ fail to find its place within this outpouring of ideas and endeavors? Like so many other priests of his generation, he was, indeed, talking about total immersion. "In the seminary, but also in the Church at large, priests were talking about immersing themselves totally in the masses. Their ideal was to become an integral part of suffering mankind even at the risk of losing themselves. That inspired me greatly; we were living in the hope of really becoming the poor. For me, this was one of the most intense times of my life in the church. During those years, I witnessed priests leaving their rectory to go to live in underprivileged neighborhoods... Throughout France, I saw priests leaving everything. So my ministry began in an extraordinary atmosphere.

"We wanted to be present among the suffering. When I asked my bishop if I could join the Mission de France, it was not to get involved in militant actions there but to be in communion with a poor population. Most of us longed to plunge deeply into this population in order to find our way back to the very substance of the Church and to discover who we were ourselves. We wanted to bring the Good News to the poor as Christ had ordered us to and, at the same time, to carry on what Christ had already accomplished; 'The poor are hearing the Good News.' We believed, and I still believe, that the evangelization of the poor was already achieved. We wanted to plunge even deeper into suffering mankind, realizing that, in this way, we would rediscover the Church in all its truth and splendor. We wanted to live our priesthood in the very heart of the Church of the Poor."

"One of the most intense times of my life in the Church ..." Did this crucial time of enthusiastic unity not last, then? Let us follow Father Joseph into his first parishes. In 1946, he was appointed assistant priest to an already elderly parish priest of Tergnier. His assignment included the parish of Vouël and the housing development for railroad employees of Quessy. Former parishioners remember, "He was young; he was with an old priest who wasn't in good health. You might as well say that, to young people of those days, he came as a breath of fresh air, and what a breath! He was very demanding, both with himself and with others. He had nothing of his own; he was already very close to the poorest."

"He was a pioneer; with him, we had to shift into high gear! It was when the statue of Our Lady of Boulogne passed by during a procession that we began to discover the deep love he felt for the Virgin Mary. He was the one who had organized everything. He managed to find and motivate about ten men to pull the float. It was a float with real tires! The church was full of flowers; this was a real celebration. For people like us, this was fantastic... Joseph had put everything into motion so that the procession of the Virgin through the streets and into the church would be a real success and a grand event!"

Still, in Father Joseph's eyes, far too many railroad employees were absent from this celebration. The next Christmas, with the children of Quessy, he built a huge nativity scene, which became famous. The Virgin and the Child, seated on an Alsatian-style float were surrounded by familiar landscapes from Tergnier, such as train cars, factories, and well-known local characters. The scene carried this message: "He came to his own, but his own did not recognize him." "At that time, the scene almost caused a scandal, but not for the young people. And everyone came to see it!"

The parishioners also remember the young assistant priest who was always on the spot when bad luck, trouble, or death struck. "He makes sure that everyone pitches in; pledges to defray funeral costs are taken when families have a hard time to make ends meet. Because of him, people take turns day and night staying with young parents who have lost a child. Even though he had nothing for himself, he came to see us often after father had left us, and he never showed up empty-handed. When he left us, he didn't have any furniture; he was using crates as tables and chairs. We had even given him a going-away present; he could have used that to buy something."

"He was living with a priest who was much older than he was. The person who was looking after the house was in the habit of keeping it constantly locked up. We teen-agers had to climb in through the window to go to meetings. The only room that he lived in was never heated. Moved by his missionary zeal but also by the friendship that people felt for him in the railroad company's housing development, he sometimes came home too late for the meal in the rectory. Often, there was nothing left to eat. Fortunately, in our area, no house was ever closed to him."

For lack of a meeting room and for lack of an open and available rectory, Father Joseph had to start the Young Christian Workers' Association from scratch in a laundry room. The young ladies got together in the basement of a haberdashery. As for catechism classes, he obtained an out-of-service train car from the French National Railroads. Railroad employees set it up for him, and he gathered children together there. Soon the train car also became a rallying point and a meeting room for adults. Even now, retired railroad employees recall an extraordinary period. "For him, all people were equal, and all were Jesus' brothers and sisters. He always used to say, 'You ought to unite.' He was not just an average priest; he did everything, according to what his heart and faith told him. It's hard to believe that this was forty years ago! He was never understood by the Church, not even by some Christians."

## What Sacrifices Will Reaching The Poorest Require?

Did the railroad employees of the company-built housing development of Quessy, who were used to seeing him coming and going, sometimes have trouble understanding him themselves?

"I have never forgotten those years when, as a young assistant priest in Tergnier, along with the railroad employees, I took part in their strikes. I used to ask the women who stood on their doorsteps in the housing development, 'Why aren't you out there with your husbands? Aren't you the first to be concerned by their struggle?' I remember emptying the parish storage room, which I had had a lot of difficulty filling with supplies for summer camps. I distributed sugar, noodles, and rice to families on strike.

"But from these first experiences as assistant priest in an environment of workers on strike, I learned that by joining with the strikers, by stirring up their wives, without fully realizing it, I found myself separated from the most underprivileged workers. Unskilled manual laborers and by far the most unfortunate, they were employed at the most repugnant, least stable and most poorly paid tasks in factories such as Japy in Beautor. Obviously, the few advantages won by the railroad employees did not concern them. They were not in the same category of workers, and their situation worsened dramatically. Without quite realizing it at that moment, I was led to spend more and more time with them and their families, who were wounded and humiliated to be left out or considered unworthy that others fight on their behalf.

"This came as a lesson to me who, ever since my years in the Seminary, was in the habit of trying to be present first of all in underprivileged housing developments. I had thrown myself into the struggle. I had found both a place for myself and personal fulfillment there, and now, suddenly, I was no longer altogether on the side of the poorest. Does Jesus' answer[4] to Satan in the desert not mean that we must take these workers as a starting point for all our struggles, allowing both ourselves and — apparently — the efficiency of any working-class struggle to be weakened by them?"

Looking back later, Father Joseph would add, "The Church has something to say about labor unions and politics. Still, it absolutely cannot talk about them like others do. A Christian must go to

4 Christ's answer to Satan's questions, as recounted in Mark 4, 1-11, was always the resounding "No" by which He refused to be led away from accomplishing His Father's will by Satan's enticements to give in to the temptations of power, popularity and domination. On page 22 of *Blessed Are You the Poor!*, Father Joseph offers us this reflection on the meaning of the confrontation between Christ and Satan. "It is this very Jesus, close to the extremely poor for having known and experienced their sorrows, whom we are going to meet again in the desert at the scene of the Temptation. Sooner or later temptation was bound to come. Eventually the Son must, in His turn and of His own free will, choose the design conceived by His Father. And in order to pledge total obedience, He must choose with full knowledge of the facts. Such was Christ's choice, one that seems almost unbelievable and unacceptable even to many Christians today. The Lord knew the condition He chose. The hour of the Temptation was not only the moment in which to choose the situation He would embrace in the world: it was the hour in which Jesus deliberately chose the men and women who had to bear that situation. Among the crowd of the poor, Jesus' preference would go to those whom no one but He would choose, the crippled, the lepers, the men of ill repute, the prostitutes, the lame, all those whom the poor themselves tend to ignore and who therefore are the most wretched and vulnerable."

the very end of encounters with human beings. He can never be satisfied with encounters that do not reach all human beings, the poorest as well as the richest... A Christian cannot consider either politics or labor unions without referring to that hidden part of the Church, its most painful part, this 'under sea level' part that the world does not see. A believer should always answer calls for more justice by asking, 'Justice for whom?'"

Are we to believe that, in Tergnier-Vouël, those who were then young people have understood? In February 1988, the newspaper *Aisne Nouvelle* writes, "Forty years later, they recall his energy, his faith, his strength of character, his love for the 'least', and his sense of sharing, which went so far as to give all he had." Those concerned will tell it in their own way. "There was no use beating around the bush. We absolutely had to do something and especially something that we had never done before! He took us up to the Cross. We all set out anyway; we would have gone anywhere with him. He never felt the need to brag, but there was in him a real need to move. Things had to fly!" One of those who speaks that way asserts, "If we don't continue what he set in motion, he's likely to come back. He only spent a little time with us, but our memory of him is still so vivid that it helps us to think and to reach out to support others, in spite of our own difficulties." They have set up an organization for the disabled. "You see, we raised the seeds that he sowed."

# Chapter Six

# "AN EXCEPTIONAL PRIEST"

### Dhuizel-la-Jolie: "He Is Bringing Us Brand-New Ideas."

Only later would the parishioners of Tergnier realize how fragile the health of their assistant priest actually was. He paid no attention to it himself. It was his friend, Father Bach, who had known about his health ever since the Second World War, who worried about it. "*I* saw him as he really was. He was exhausted by all he was doing because he just had no extra reserves. He had always been weak because he was brought up in poverty. This affects your whole life. Tuberculosis came from his childhood, that's for sure, as well as from the way he lived when he was in the Aisne. He used to live with the bare necessities."

In fact, in 1948, when Father Joseph asked his bishop to let him spend some time in the Mission de France Seminary in Lisieux, he got meningitis there. He recovered from it and left with an assignment to preach in Saint-Dizier, in Reims, and in Bordeaux on behalf of diocesan missionaries. Only a little later, he came down with a serious case of tuberculosis. In 1949, he had to be driven on a stretcher to Angers to attend funeral services for the mother whom he had loved as only a child in bottomless poverty can love his mother without having the words to tell her. It would take him a year to recover completely from his illness, but he had trouble just biding his time. He learned to look after the other patients in the sanatorium; then Father Bach welcomed him as a guest to Pressigny in the Haute-Marne.

"He took care of religious services. People just loved him. On Sundays, crowds came to listen to him. His sermons made him famous, and he was in great demand. He knew how to talk to people. Thirty-five years later, when he died, I got phone calls because people had kept unforgettable memories of him." Many children would remember their first communion especially well, because he had his own inimitable way of preparing everyone for it. "Kids had to find pictures and examples from everyday life." Many of them have held on to the notebook that he asked them to make. Father Bach, who heard him give "a fantastic sermon," asked him to come back each year.

Still, "all good things come to an end. He left on a hitchhiking pilgrimage to Rome and, on his return from this adventure, went back to Soissons." Why did he go to Soissons rather than to Lisieux? In Lisieux, he had found a friend, Father Emeriau, professor of sociology and of the ethics of theology. However, it seemed that this was not the place where the young priest would find the path plunging "even deeper into suffering mankind," which he had been hoping for since his days in the seminary. His bishop suggested that he settle down in a rural community that was both poor and dechristianized. "Unless you go, this parish won't have a priest any longer." He was appointed parish priest of Dhuizel in charge of two more nearby parishes and several isolated villages. Let us listen to what the priests of the diocese, the former mayor, and the inhabitants themselves have to say about him.

"It is true that, upon his arrival, he had a lot of statues removed from the church; that surprised people." This was exactly what Father Joseph was hoping to accomplish: to show people, even if it meant surprising them, that believers would not abandon the house and the presence of God to the solitary surveillance of a few plaster saints. He mustered into work young people who often could not come before nightfall. Renovations therefore were done in the evening. "They carted out one wheelbarrow after another. So people wondered: what are they digging for? The priest must have found some treasure." There was so little treasure, in fact, that Father Bach had to help finance the work. "This was when I noticed that, from an artistic point of view, he had good taste. He fully renovated his church. I was helping him financially because he was always completely broke. However, he was an expert in renovation." This was how a wooden altar dedicated to the Virgin made its appearance, followed by a large carved stone, which would be used as the main altar. Suddenly, one Sunday, it was there and the priest celebrated holy mass in front of an astonished congregation. He also invited his elder brother, who was a wood sculptor, to restore a seventeenth century statue.

The enthusiastic hands of young people from three villages turned the church into a wonderful work of art. In a region whose inhabitants observed, "We had completely forgotten about all that," Father Joseph brought back the famous nativity scenes, as well as first communions and confirmations. As he himself would say: "The poor need signs. The Church should not move forward without them." A lady of the parish recalls: "What struck people the most were the nativity scenes. The first year, with the children, he represented New York City in one of them. They made skyscrapers out of cardboard. At the city's feet, there was the Christ child, cast aside and abandoned by modern society. The year after, he had us construct a huge globe representing the earth. We had to outfit our dolls to represent children from all over the world, and they had to hold hands stretching around the earth."

As for the rectory, a small one-story building with only one room fit to live in, it was quite a different matter. Besides the restoration of the Lord's house, seasonal agricultural laborers were the other concern keeping this priest busy. They were Belgian, Polish, Italian, Spanish, or Portuguese. They were underpaid and shabbily housed in dilapidated homes with broken windows. Father Joseph accepted a job working beside them, thereby creating considerable uneasiness among a handful of wealthy grain and beet growers. He began hoeing, thinning, and transplanting beets, tasks that were far beyond his physical strength, but that he nevertheless carried out completely. When they saw seasonal workers gather in the rectory in the evening, the farmers spoke out in protest, "This is not the right place for him." The rectory seemed to become a rallying-point for the down-and-out of the whole area. "Basically," as a former parishioner said thoughtfully, "he came to save what was lost."

One day, a young man, whom the district police chief will soon come looking for, stops by the clergyman's home. Two district courts have issued warrants for the youth's arrest. When questioned, the priest, standing on his doorstep where everyone can hear him, answers calmly: "I know. Late Saturday night, I drove this young man to Belgium." Was this not going a bit too far? Looking back, the former mayor of Dhuizel makes allowances: "This priest was a man with a big heart. Giving help with no strings attached to desperate people was something of an obsession with him. He put this first in all his endeavors, shaking up people he considered to be unaware of the problems — at the risk, if need be, of alienating them."

A former colleague from the diocese tells us, "In those days, his sermons didn't beat around the bush. He used to talk about landowners who were not always kind nor fair to workers. Still, he never mentioned anyone by name and he treated everyone with great consideration. During the elevation of the Blessed Sacrament, he could sometimes be heard to say, 'working class, working class;' just as, at other times, while holding up the eucharistic host, he would repeat, 'Justice, truth, love and peace.' One day, I happened by during mass. He was all alone, facing an imaginary audience, and I heard him say, 'Ah, my poor Lord, I am praying to you for all these scoundrels.'"

Meanwhile, the landowners did not stop saying, "But this is not the right place for him here. In our region of high-yield farming there's no such thing as an urban working class." Was he in the right place indeed, this priest whose lodgings were closely watched after he had extended the hand of fellowship to a population group that the rest of the community mistrusted? Where did he belong, this priest who went out hoeing beets and who could be seen in the evening working in his own garden in shorts? Was he where he ought to be, this priest, who, during the celebration of confirmation, got the bishop invited into the most wretched household of the parish? Many who knew him then thought, "It was too small for him here. Just imagine, with all his resources of intelligence and broadmindedness..." *He* himself never spoke this way about Dhuizel, which he had baptized "Dhuizel, the beautiful." His three parishes did not seem to be too small to him. "A single one would have been enough for me if I could have believed that there I had reached the rock bottom of my plunge into humanity." But with whom could he share the anxiety of not yet having come to the end of this plummeting path?

His colleagues like him; some feel great concern for him. The Dean of Braine recounts, "I knew Joseph in 1955 and 1956. There were six priests, including himself, in the deanery. Upon his arrival, the superior of the seminary told me, 'One of these six is a rare pearl, an extremely talented and highly original man. His background is surprising. His father is Polish; his mother, Spanish. He has great gifts of the mind and heart and great commitment. He is an exceptional priest.' The vicar general would tell me furthermore, 'Be very flexible with him in your meetings. If he comes in the middle of the day or only for a meal, take him as he is.' There was agreement on this point: what we wanted was to incorporate him fully into our team. I used to say to those who sometimes complained: 'He is bringing us brand-new ideas.' His originality would sometimes rub parishioners and even us the wrong way, but he was just telling the truth because he was truly a priest."

*Father Joseph, circa 1957.*

Father Edward Polyn adds that not all of his colleagues could understand that. "Our advantage over the others was that we had worked on the catechism text with him. Putting together our own catechism was a revolutionary experience. We worked hours together, very closely. The other priests didn't know him as well; all they noticed was that he was not like them. Many thought that all he had on his mind was working, that he wanted to be a working priest. Personally, I believe that he had something entirely different in mind. He was looking, thinking, and waiting. He took part in all the meetings of our theology course. He was also traveling; he wanted to see things on his own.

"Once there were fifteen of us at table, eating and discussing together, and he said to us, 'Do you want me to tell you what the Church is? The Church is a bitch, that's what she is! You don't know what a bitch is? It is quite simply someone who takes advantage of you, who makes your wheels spin. Still, when all is said and done, you are so attracted to her that you don't want to leave her. She may be a bitch, but she's my mother, and I love her.' The Church was sacred to him. Still, people who had reached a certain age might well wonder: 'What kind of a priest is he?' Nevertheless, he was not emptying our churches; quite the opposite. People went to listen to him, even if it was in order to criticize him. Of course, he was not at all a crowd-pleaser. With all his outspokenness, he had wit and refinement. It was amazing to see this kind of revolutionary priest who was so tenderhearted and who always remained the priest for one and all."

Another priest emphasizes, "He had enormous sensitivity and, when he got angry, he was unhappy afterward, and he immediately cleared the air. His outbursts of anger quite often expressed some suffering. At a certain point, to be sure, he couldn't keep quiet."

## Where Are the Oppressed?

Obviously, his colleagues are both very friendly and very bewildered. What could the future hold for such a non-conformist priest? "He brought revolution to us long before Vatican II; it was fantastic but disturbing. His rectory was so bare, like everywhere else he lived; but it was always full of people — a real rallying point. In the church too, everything seemed to change. He accepted girls as well as boys as altar-servers. He restored the solemnity of confirmation and of the profession of faith, almost like an ordination with all the children lying down on their stomachs on the church floor. It was true that he never did things half-way. That's why there were people who admired him, others who grumbled, and still others who criticized him fiercely."

Now what should we think about the journeys that Father Joseph used to set out on? He made it clear. "I'm not going on a pilgrimage; I'm going to have a look." That was how he took Father Bach along with him to the Rhineland. They went to pray at Maria

Laach, of course, but mainly to visit a country left in ruins. Then, Father Bach took him along to the Middle East. He celebrated mass on the site of Jesus' tomb, then moved on to discover areas of extreme poverty. "Human misery haunted him. He always related with such ease to everyone; very few people make such easy contact." The next destination would be Spain, where he asked his companions to make a long detour through the province of Murcia. He had heard that, in this region, teachers had neither books nor notebooks for their classes. "In Father Joseph's opinion, that was another form of need and deprivation. He made us wait three days." A little later, the small group visited some sanctuaries, laden with statues and precious stones. His companions spoke about corrupt practices: dire poverty on the one hand, diamonds on the other. How could they understand why Father Joseph got angry. "What do you mean? Nothing is too beautiful for the Blessed Virgin! Quite frankly, this is all perfectly normal; all these treasures are for the Lord."

"Father Joseph," as Father Emeriau now fondly recalls, "did not have a traditional priestly calling. He was still looking for his direction in life. Most of the time, the priests who came to the Mission de France did not follow a traditional calling either. Still, even among them, Father Joseph stood out a little. His character showed even more boldness."

In 1955, the superior of the Braine seminary had stated more simply: "He is an exceptional priest." The vicar-general had added: "Take him as he is." How can one keep one's heart from aching when thinking back on the young priest who, in 1946, had seen his priesthood begin "in an extraordinary atmosphere"? After six years in Dhuizel and nine years of priesthood, how had the feeling of a deeply shared aspiration turned into such solitude? Father Joseph himself, however, did not think of it in these terms.

"Nothing had changed; we were all following the same path. We were all searching, but we were not all searching in the same way. We were not starting from, nor talking about, the same reality. As for me, I had to start from where I was born, with the experience and outlook that extreme poverty had given me. I did not know any more than they did where this would lead me." With his passion for history as well as for unity, and with his faithfulness to the Church, he would always consider himself an heir, never a dissident, and even less a revolutionary. He would remind us of the wealth of new initiatives created in the Church at this time and in which he took part: the rediscovery of the daily life of dechristianized population groups ("but are they really dechristianized?"), the realization that it was as if the poor had been weeded out of history, that the major problem of the separation between different social groups lay in culture, the longing to "live with" rather than to reclaim territory for the Church, the passion for human beings as well as for communities, and the determination to forego basic security in order to connect with real people and communities, the participation of the laity in the Church's ministry. Father Joseph took part in all these strides forward with enthusiasm even if it was sometimes tinged with sadness.

Indeed, he also noticed the confusion concerning the issue of who were the "oppressed," the "underprivileged masses," the "suffering masses," the "disinherited," the "working classes who lack all basic security." When his colleagues talked about a community-based spirituality, just who were the members of this community? When they yearned to share in extreme poverty, whose condition did they have in mind? Where were the very poorest? What position and role were they given in these projects? What were the Church's and society's ambitions on their behalf? Were we sure that we were not stopping half way on our journey while Jesus, the wretched Lord, was waiting for us farther on down the road? These were the questions that were haunting him, because, in his opinion, they were haunting the Church. "The Church knows that there will always be even poorer people in whom Jesus becomes flesh and blood. The Church knows that it cannot rest before reaching them, since it is compelled to reach out even farther and deeper. Would our suffering as priests, in fact, not be that at the end of our lives the Lord might say to us, 'I was dwelling in those people; I was in that shack, or in that emergency housing project. I was this family paralyzed by anxiety; I was these children deprived of learning. You passed by close to me, and you did not recognize me; you did not even stay a while.'"

Where are the very poorest? One day, in 1956, Bishop Douillard summons Father Joseph. "There's this emergency housing camp near Paris. They came to ask for advice. Chaplains don't seem to be able to stay on there. What do you think about that? You may go and look around. You are free to come back whenever you wish." Father Joseph, the open, spontaneous man of action, able to make quick decisions, is in fact a very cautious person. "It is the reflex of a poor person. Poor people like myself always have to keep one step ahead of misfortune." He returns to Dhuizel to think things over. He pays a short visit to the emergency housing camp of Noisy-le-Grand without introducing himself to anyone. Then he goes to see his lifelong friend, Father Bach. Without mentioning the emergency housing camp, he just asks him to stop over in Dhuizel. "Tell me what you think about my parish today."

"He asked me to come see his parish. I went there one Sunday when I had found someone to substitute for me. I attended his mass, unannounced, with two other people whom I had brought with me from Pressigny. They told me, 'This is not the right kind of parish for a man like him. An energetic man like him doesn't belong in a parish where no one comes to church." He was standing there; the children were singing; he delivered a wonderful sermon. I said to him, 'Poor Joseph, listen to me. You shouldn't stay here; you ought to take on something more challenging.' Then he told me about the emergency housing camp of Noisy-le-Grand, and I replied that it would be just right for him. I didn't really know this camp, but I did know him and his lifetime experience with grinding poverty. He listened to me, and he left."

Father Joseph would keep a rock-solid friendship with his colleagues from the diocese of Soissons to whom he would remain devoted all his life. "They guided my first steps; they are my friends." Thirty years later, they would say about Father Joseph, "Certainly, you were exceptional. Not without cause, you sometimes exasperated the conformists and the prosperous. Yet, with the stubbornness of a mule, you remained faithful to yourself, to your origins, and to the vocation to which the Lord had called you."

## Chapter Seven

# THE EMERGENCY HOUSING CAMP, OR RETURNING TO THE PATHS OF SHAME

### "On That Day, I Went Back into Wretchedness"

"My bishop had suggested that I spend some time among these very poor families and then choose whether or not I wanted to stay with them. So I went for six months first and, during the early part of my stay, I mingled with the Companions of Emmaus.[5] I worked with them, I lived like them and, since they were doing repair work in the Camp of Noisy-le-Grand, I was able to approach families who had found shelter there.

"I arrived on a plateau called the 'Château de France' on July 14, 1956. The sun was giving off a scorching heat, and the alleys were deserted. There was no one outside. Facing this emptiness, I thought: in the past, springs, road junctions, a church-tower, or a trade united people. Here the families are gathered together by extreme poverty. It came to me like an inspiration. I knew that I was no longer facing a commonplace situation of relative poverty (as one used to say then) or personal problems. I was dealing with mass poverty. From the very start, I felt that I was facing my people. This cannot be explained. It just happened.

---

5 The Companions of Emmaus (known in French as *les Compagnons d'Emmaus*) are communities of homeless men first established and chartered by Abbé Pierre in 1954. Members of the Emmaus Community of Noisy-le-Grand helped to set up Marabout tents, which sheltered the first families who came to Noisy-le-Grand seeking refuge from the terrible winter of 1954. Often working as ragpickers to provide for their communities, members are invited to live by Abbé Pierre's ideal of helping people even more destitute than they.

"From that very moment, my life took a new direction. The blinding poverty that spread before my eyes in a stifling heat and absolute silence had me caught in a trap. It was on July 14, 1956, that I signed my fate, even though I was able to wait until November 11 to settle for good in Noisy-le-Grand. Even on that November 11, I still kept my old parish anyway. I went there every Saturday and Sunday. Born a child of poverty and having remained a man of poverty deep inside myself, I had learned to believe in everything, to dare to do anything, but still to keep supplies stored away somewhere, such as a pear for my thirst and a piece of stale bread in my pocket. There's not a single poor person who would not do likewise. My own mother did it. She kept a spare pair of shoes for her children or a spare pair of pants. She told me, 'Joseph, if you refuse what they bring you today, then when you do need something, they will have given it all away to someone else.' I kept my old parish for several months, like my mother would always keep a pair of shoes, just to be on the safe side."

"I signed my fate," said Father Joseph. For it did take his own signature, no one was forcing him. Only one man, Father Bach, had encouraged him, and we will find out later that many others did the opposite. Then again, did he not have every reason not to become involved in such a hellish adventure?

Even during the early years of his priesthood, Father Joseph could with a clear conscience already have stopped half way, as he used to say. "In my opinion, a priest is someone who belongs to his people. He mixes with them to the point of blending in with them completely. During the early years of my priesthood, I did achieve this kind of symbiosis with the families in my parishes. These were the happiest years of my life." "He's a real priest," his colleagues used to say, even if they did not always understand him. What more could one ask for? We only know that Father Joseph did ask for more from his priesthood. He was not looking for more satisfaction or happiness, but for more faithfulness to the wretched Jesus Christ, crucified as an outlaw.

"No one can be a priest without a sort of deep-seated intimacy with Jesus Christ. This means a bond with him, not as a symbol, but as a living reality reflecting what the world is going through and what the poorest around us are expressing and hoping for. A priest is bound, one way or another, to want to shape his life within the life of Jesus Christ; otherwise, he does not remain a priest. The life of the Lord in the world is that of the child born in a place where only children of such marginal people as the shepherds could be born. His life is that of a penniless, homeless, expelled family; that of an unemployed man belittled even in his suffering and whose pain, people say, is very much his own fault."

Later, when he would speak, with both the love and the familiarity that we have witnessed, about his Lord in the hour of Temptation, was it not because he himself wanted to follow Jesus there as well? Concerning July 14, 1956, he would say toward the end of his life, "On that day, I went back into wretchedness. In those women, I recognized my mother; those children were my brothers and my sister." But did he not also assert that anyone who has escaped from relentless poverty cannot want to go back to it?

"A person born in a poverty-stricken family, in a milieu so poor as to suffer constant anxiety and humiliation, cannot wish to remain in that condition. Neither the feeling of belonging there, nor the conviction that he owes solidarity to his own in their struggle for a better life, can make him accept being held in contempt. This runs counter to his nature and his very calling as a human being. Poverty, material deprivation, oppression inflicted by those who are stronger than you — these are hard to bear. What is truly insufferable, however, is being despised and continuously reminded that one is an inferior and utterly useless being. Fourth World families bring this home to us day by day. Being treated as a person without dignity even by one's own is virtually intolerable. 'People treat us like nobodies. Are we dogs, to be kicked around as we are at the town hall?'

"This is where the difference lies between poverty and total deprivation. A person in extreme poverty suffers an unbearable situation, being considered negligible or, worse, a harmful being who should never have been born; while deep inside he still knows he is a person. To long for dignity, to dream of being someone and yet to be denied this even by those hardly better off than oneself: the neighbors, the grocer, the postman — that is extreme poverty. And that is what makes the difference between poverty and exclusion."

In 1956, Father Joseph goes back to that borderline. Does he really have to cross it again? Even in Dhuizel, he has never lost touch with the facts of life. All through life, he will keep this sensitivity of the very poor who read in people's eyes the astonishment, the contempt their tongues do not put into words. He knows that many people see him as "exceptional." Until now, however, his confidence and good humor have always outshone his feeling of humiliation and shyness. He has been following his own path in life with serenity. Certainly, his mother has rooted in him this advice all the very poor give to their children: "Above all, Joseph, don't make yourself conspicuous." If Joseph does make himself conspicuous all the same, it is only because, on behalf of the very poor, he often cannot do otherwise. Then again, until now he could in a way afford to do so, because he did have some basic security, namely a recognized position in the Church. From now on, this security will elude him. He knows that people are trying to find him a job as assistant priest. He will be appointed to the parish team of Noisy-le-Grand, put in charge of the chaplaincy of the "Italian Nuns" of the Order of Frances Cabrini. The emergency housing camp of Noisy-le-Grand is not a parish even if it includes six times as many families as Dhuizel. Neither does it represent a chaplaincy in its own right. However, what Father Joseph is going to discover in this camp makes him realize that, unless it is built on a solid foundation, the future of any action he undertakes will remain uncertain.

## Only One Answer to Extreme Poverty: "These Families Will Climb the Steps of the Vatican, the Elysée Palace, and the United Nations."

Just what exactly does it mean to "blend in" with this people of outcasts, trapped on a deserted plateau beyond the city limits of Paris? For one brief moment, Father Joseph has dreamed once again of totally immersing himself in the masses. However, he does feel that his life would no longer be altogether like that. "Ever since that day, I have been haunted by the idea that this people would never escape from extreme poverty as long as it was not welcomed as a whole, as a people, wherever the rest of humanity held discussions and debates. I promised myself that if I stayed, I would do whatever was needed so that these families would be able to climb the steps of the Vatican, the Elysée Palace, and the United Nations."

Father Joseph had returned to the deep poverty of his own family, to the exclusion of families from the Saint-Nicolas neighborhood, and to his whole childhood filled with anguish and humiliation. How could he fail to get involved? Was this not why he had been following his Lord? But Father Joseph was frightened too. He had no resources and no basic security. "Joining in the fight for the excluded is not that simple. One does not defend the interests of individuals scattered here and there: a drunken mother, a wretched old woman, a puny boy. I had to meet them as one people and to discover that I was one of them. As an adult, I had to recognize myself in these kids who live in the housing projects surrounding our cities and in these unemployed youths crying with rage. They perpetuate the extreme poverty of my childhood, and they remind me of the persistence of a people in rags.

"It is within our power to put an end to this everlasting condition. Extreme poverty will not exist tomorrow if we accept the task of helping these youths to gain awareness of their people, to change their violence into a lucid struggle, to arm themselves with love, hope, and knowledge in order to bring to a close the struggle against ignorance, hunger, handouts, and exclusion.

"However, this will not just be the business of governments. It will be the concern, first and foremost, of men and women wanting to walk with a rejected people and to link their own lives with theirs, sometimes at the cost of leaving everything behind to share in their fate."

Now, Father Joseph was well aware that linking one's life to the life of such a devastated population group would appear to be sheer madness in the eyes of the world. He always thought of Jesus at the hour of Temptation, but how reassuring could this image be at the moment when it seemed to be his turn to make a binding choice? "Can we be anything but bewildered when we imagine the complete reversal Jesus brings about in the course of the world's history? From this moment, nothing will ever be the same again; everything becomes *equally* possible to all, be they rich, or poor and excluded. Fear, diffidence, and infinite gratitude mingle in my heart because of all I have learned from the poor in my youth and ever since." These would be Father Joseph's words thirty years later. For the time being, he cannot yet measure the reversal that he, too, will have to carry out. But he is afraid because he foresees that he is going back into suffering without knowing whether he will overcome it. He foresees the weight of the burden awaiting him, just by counting the number of ill-inspired interventions to which the families of the Camp have to submit. "The emergency housing camp was hidden from the world's eyes, but it was like the town square to the charitable organizations of those days: a soup kitchen, organizations promoting adoption, distributions of clothing — twenty-seven charitable organizations, doing whatever they wanted."

"On that day, I went back into wretchedness..." Guided by his tactfulness, Father Joseph did not specify just how intense this wretchedness was. Guided by a concern not to downplay the outpouring of good will brought forth by Abbé Pierre's appeal,[6] he did not say how much this situation resembled the condition his own family had experienced. Just as in the past, it was not caused merely by the indifference — not to say the coldhearted cruelty — of a society toward its weakest members. It also stemmed from the ill-advised and often

*The Camp of Noisy-le-Grand.*

[6] Abbé Pierre's appeal was launched toward the French and international communities in February 1954 after several homeless adults had been found dead of frostbite under Paris bridges. This campaign was so successful at fundraising that Abbé Pierre, priest, member of the French Parliament and founder of the Emmaus Communities, was able to buy some land in Noisy-le-Grand (see note 2), where he had tents put up to provide temporary shelter and relief to some homeless families. Ill health prevented him from continuing to follow this project closely.

bungling good will of people who had not experienced extreme poverty themselves. It also came from organizations that, out of sheer ignorance, repeated the time-worn actions that the non-poor had been applying to the most underprivileged people without asking them for advice, hearing their refusal, or imagining their despair. In the Camp of Noisy-le-Grand, Father Joseph rediscovered the paths of shame: "The receding shadow of a woman carrying her chamber pot to the only public latrine... children picking through trash cans, early in the morning, looking for crusts of bread ... Chantal brings me a piece of paper on which her mother has written, 'Father, my children have had nothing to eat since yesterday.' The entire population has the mind-set of starving people. With ups and downs, they have always lived as outcasts. They are forced to beg." How could these paths of shame be removed forever and replaced by paths of honor?

Some people may have taken for granted that Father Joseph would simply take over from those who had gone before him in this place. Yet how could a man, so shaped and schooled by the extreme poverty into which he had been born, adopt and sponsor as his own the plans and projects of people from very different backgrounds, seemingly the opposite of his own? Was the contrary not more likely to happen? By becoming an actor in the history of the families of the emergency housing camp, by blending in with them, was he not destined to reverse the course of that history? He could not just pick up its loose ends. Given what he was, he could only throw himself, body and soul, as a roadblock across its path.

Today, we realize that Father Joseph's total immersion in the Camp of Noisy-le-Grand was going to embody very poor people's total refusal of the fate that their fellow citizens, even through their charitable activities, had imposed on them. It was going to give life to the refusal of the fate that had been imposed on their parents and grandparents and that could in no way be accepted any longer. Later Father Joseph would express this refusal in a now famous motto: "Extreme poverty cannot be relieved; we can only put an end to it." Still, to what hope could one hold fast? "This Camp is the hell that people in their ignorance create for the poor. The hell that Jesus had overcome has been reconstructed by human beings." There must be a way to get out of this hell, and in order to emerge from it a whole people will have to stand up on its own feet. What resources are available? What is the value of the few sparks of hope that the families have kept alive in the midst of the overall breakdown that has stranded them in this place? What is the value of their muted refusal to be considered unworthy, the refusal that others do not even hear, but that Father Joseph recognizes because he has witnessed it in his own mother? The families are barely able to show any proof of it, after all the snubs and wounds inflicted on them.

In 1956, Father Joseph walked into an encampment of families that was not just another underprivileged area. Its very hardships made it unique in its suffering. Society had persisted in treating these families as aid recipients, as "hopeless cases," rather than recognizing in them a people longing for honor, independence, responsibility, and rights. On his part, Father Joseph had not yet measured the full scope of the task he was taking on. Yet this time, he did know that he had reached the very bottom of human misery. He was too familiar with this relentless poverty not to have some inkling of what was waiting for him: the fear and hesitation on the part of the families, and the misunderstanding and opposition on the part of society. He knew too much about what he was getting into not to be afraid — he who had been acquainted with fear throughout his childhood.

When on November 11, 1956, Father Joseph moved into a shack in this place called the "Château de France," he moved back into anxiety, but he did so at peace with himself. Could anyone understand? Again people would say that he was not in the right place. "This camp is not a place where a priest should live," was what the director of a charitable organization wrote, adding, "There's too much violence and degradation there." Father Joseph would say about this period of his life, "I started with no chance of winning, but that was my good luck. I had nothing, not a thing to fall back on at all. My only resource was trust."

## Chapter Eight

# THE FIRST ASSOCIATION: AN ACT OF FAITH

### Extreme Poverty — a People's Untold History

How was one supposed to understand that trust could be an essential resource in fighting poverty? Let us keep in mind that chronic poverty, in the 1950s, spread across all of France and neighboring countries. Father Joseph had discovered it while traveling in Spain, in Italy, and in the Federal Republic of Germany. In France, this poverty stood out above all in housing conditions. For the poorest families, the housing situation was still dreadful since all available decent lodgings had been taken by somewhat less deprived households. Many of the very poor were leaving the countryside, where mechanization was making agricultural laborers unneeded. These laborers found no suitable housing in cities, where employment did not develop in ways favorable to these domestic migrants anyway. Neither did industrial development benefit the most underprivileged among the urban population, who continued to earn starvation wages and to live in deplorable housing. In those days, the homeless were only the visible tip of the iceberg: a whole people from both urban and rural backgrounds was trapped underground in a kind of boundless poverty; a "people under sea level," as Father Joseph used to say. Emergency housing projects, shelters, shantytowns, and the Camp of Noisy-le-Grand set up in 1954 were ultimately the end of the road for an entire part of the French people. Victims of all-out poverty and chronic underemployment, due to their lack of training and excessively harsh living conditions, these families were constantly moving from slum to furnished hotel room, from tool shed to emergency shelter.

Father Joseph noticed what had escaped the public's attention during the ground swell of enthusiasm set in motion by Abbé Pierre. Extreme poverty had not disappeared, either in France or in Western Europe. To be sure, on account of a certain decrease in their numbers, the very poor were no longer liable to disturb their fellow citizens as before. Politicians were no longer thinking about them. Even public authorities had lost touch with the realities of poverty. By 1956, thousands of children were not getting enough to eat, yet the public failed to do any soul-searching or to ask for facts and figures. Father Joseph moved into the emergency housing camp of Noisy-le-Grand, aware that the challenge that had to be met was not so much the lack of housing as the fathomless poverty of a whole people. But he was going to have to state this case to the whole country and sometimes, even, to his Church. If he failed to do so, he could not endeavor to fight poverty as such. Surrounding society would ask him to prove that poverty actually existed and that the state of degradation and brokenness of an entire population group did deserve to be called poverty.

From now on, there will be more and more eyewitnesses of Father Joseph's life. Among them, there will be many families living in persistent poverty in different parts of the world, and we shall hear from them. But first let us listen once again to Father Bach, the unfailing friend who understood Father Joseph so well.

"I went to his place in Noisy-le-Grand. For me, this was an experience somewhat like landing on the moon. There were Quonset huts crowded with all kinds of poverty-stricken people. Even in the shack where he, himself, had to sleep, he had set up a bed for a woman with tuberculosis who was coughing day and night. I slept there too. It was nothing but a miserable shack with holes between the wallboards. There was no heating. The only luxury item was a salvaged bathtub, but you had to go fetch water at the pump. He was really an outstanding person to be living there when he could have done otherwise.

"I stayed ten days including one Sunday. I had never imagined this kind of relationship with deepest poverty. The kids used to come and look at me with wide-opened eyes, like kids who are hungry. I would buy them some bread. They would come every day to get some. Lord, how miserable it all could be. When I went home to Moselle, the only thing I had left was my return ticket, that's how deep poverty was. It was a pitiful sight. In Europe, we were no longer accustomed to that.

"It was there that I really saw that he was doing extraordinary work. He was accepted by everyone. I heard confirmations of this everywhere in the camp. No one could challenge him; even the communists or the anti-religious were all for him; he had won them all over. In 1958, winning these folks over took courage beyond the call of duty. These folks were stranded in extreme poverty, but they had found someone.

"Joseph was a godsend. He knew them all. He never had a penny, but he had a wide field of action for his heart of gold and his overflowing imagination."

It was a wider field of action than Father Bach was imagining, since it was limitless. In the midst of such deprivation, how was Father Joseph, using trust as his only resource, going to get this field to bear fruit?

Mrs. Aubert, widow of a railroad employee, who has followed the young assistant priest from Tergnier to Dhuizel to look after him, his rectory, and items used in worship, refuses to leave him alone in Noisy-le-Grand. "I had a small retirement pension; I was free; I couldn't leave him like that." She refurbishes an igloo[7] and then a little shack. With Father Bach, she is among the few eyewitnesses who have written about the period between November 1956 and December 1960. Her heart is aching too, but like Father Bach, and contrary to most people's opinion, she thinks that Father Joseph is "really in the right place." Simply, she finds living conditions unbearable for him as well as for the families.

"I used to set up a small space heater for him, which glowed weakly when it was turned on. But air used to come through cracks in the boards, and an icy chill prevailed. The bed would disappear under a little mountain of torn blankets. He had already given his own blankets away. I counted eight pieces of covers made of small squares of multicolored wool, falling off each side of the bed. He must have shivered at night because these covers, which were too

7 An igloo was the name that families of the Camp of Noisy-le-Grand gave to their 27 ft. by 30 ft. Quonset-style huts in fibrocement with no electricity, no running water and no bathrooms.

small, would slip off at the slightest movement. In the morning, I would find them on the floor."

However, Mrs. Aubert was well aware that Father Joseph's concerns were elsewhere. "When I got to the intersection of A Street (but were these puddles really a street?) I would always see at least three or four women who were waiting for the mail and welfare checks. Every day there were women there who had no money. They were complaining about having nothing to give to their children to eat. They used to buy on credit and would come to ask Father Joseph for money, but his pockets were always empty. When welfare checks came in, I think that people who received one were not about to make sacrifices. They all had to catch up for not having eaten enough for a while.

"Winter was especially hard. In every household, there were sick people needing to be hospitalized. That created additional expenses for transportation and other needs. Seeing money melt in your hands like this is an exasperating and heartbreaking experience. People who have everything they need can't understand. They used to come to the Camp to give advice: 'If I were in your shoes ...' But they were not in the families' shoes. Only Father Joseph could have spoken this way, and he did not.

"Water was also a problem. Father Joseph had pumps installed. It was even the first thing he did. If you haven't done it, you can't know what it's like to have to go fetch water in a pail, several hundred feet away, when you need so much of it, especially when you live knee-deep in the mud. Who even imagines the wasted time and the exhaustion if they have hot running water in the sink flowing easily into the sewer? When I think of all the dirty water I saw in front of the huts, the greasy water that formed little lakes combining with those in front of the neighbor's! No one could

*An "igloo" in the Camp of Noisy-le-Grand. "No one could go outside without getting their shoes stuck in the mud."*

go outside without getting their shoes stuck in the mud. In the winter, all that water made miniature skating rinks.

"Children often take care of the chores. When they do, they don't go to school. They're pulling a laundry bucket or a pail on a cart. Their feet are soaking wet in shoes that are too big for them. In winter, the pumps have to be protected with straw and old rags. The ones that don't freeze are stormed by the crowd; people have to line up in the cold and wait for their turn. Just think of all the weight being carried by weary arms and aching backs. Just think of all the frustration, too, in front of an empty pail that you have to go and fill again. This means years of chores for women and children. When will this ever end?

"Everyone knows that you pile up garbage all day long, especially if you're a family with many children. If trash isn't collected, it's at the mercy of dogs, cats, and above all rats, which scatter it all in no time. Children are going to empty trash cans anywhere; it's disgusting and unhealthy. In the summertime, rubbish is invaded by flies you can't get rid of, in spite of insecticides. It's often raining on top of it all, and you feel like you're living on a dump.

"But maybe the worst part was the free handouts that caused not only shame but also division and quarreling among the families. Since everything was free, people were dissatisfied; some felt that others were getting better service than they were.

"Women from Paris used to come to help sort out clothes, and they all interfered in other people's business. Father Joseph would ask me to get rid of anything that wasn't any good, but these ladies would step in behind me. They would put right back on the shelves whatever was torn and old-fashioned. They found it normal to give away what they no longer wanted themselves. I felt that people were dressing the poor in rags; they had to wear just anything. The things we received from everywhere were just incredible. We would get heaps of hats for old people, overcoats from before 1914, ankle-boots with buttons, baby clothes matted and yellowed with age. Shoes were a nightmare, what with broken heels and loose soles. We had to burn all of that."

Within this incongruous universe, Mrs. Aubert sees Father Joseph moving back and forth, called for from every direction. The man who had come there, filled with fear, "always finds the words, the gesture, some activity to encourage everyone. He brings people together; he lifts up hearts...

"I have often seen him, striding up and down the paths at night with long strides, his hands squeezed deep down in his cassock pockets. I have seen him looking crushed under some burden, his face riddled with anxiety. I have seen him crying, his head clasped in his hands, whenever hardship hit the Camp: children put in foster care, the kindergarten burning down, all those fires where people lost everything, or youths taken away with handcuffs on their wrists. I have also seen him, livid with anger, his voice giving vent to his frustration over a messed-up job. He was fully a priest in church and fully a man everywhere else, with all the passion that this involves and all the fighting against so much injustice."

With thirty years' hindsight, Mrs. Aubert also says in 1987, "He is just as sensitive as ever to extreme poverty, even though his work is no longer the same today; he is just as enthusiastic. Everything began with the families, everything depended on them, and it is the families who have changed."

## Restoring the Right to Freedom of Opinion and of Association

What exactly did happen to make the families change? Father Joseph says, "I had to live with the families first. Gradually, certain realities forced themselves upon me. The first one was self-denial. I had known poverty when I was a country priest. During the first months after my arrival in my parish in Dhuizel, I did not have much to eat. I had come there with little luggage, and for a long time I had to eat out of my cooking pans. Still, all this was only skin-deep deprivation. There were always people around me ready to help me out. In Noisy-le-Grand, the deprivation I experienced was genuine because all the families living there were enduring the same hardships. I had no way of escaping. This made my solidarity with the Camp's inhabitants very genuine.

"Then something else forced its way into my mind. I remember a single mother who arrived at nightfall with her five children. I had nothing to offer her except half an igloo-hut, which meant a living area of seventeen by fifteen feet of packed dirt. I was trying to imagine what my own mother would have done. She would have gone to the town hall and begun a sit-in in the entrance, declaring, 'I won't move until you provide me with a home.' The idea of having to force society to shoulder its responsibilities never left my mind after that evening."

So the question became how to go about forcing a society, oblivious to the injustice of persistent poverty within its boundaries, to shoulder its responsibilities. And what was it responsible for? Had we not established the welfare state; had we not entered into an era of prosperity for all? If some families had nothing, who was responsible for this situation? Were their shortcomings not obvious? A people in chronic poverty? Were they not rather a people lacking willpower? Had this priest not been nicknamed long ago "the priest of the riffraff"?

The fight against persistent poverty was inevitably turning into a fight for honor, for the right to an historical identity, and for the right to express oneself and to speak on one's own behalf. Father Joseph did the only thing that was practical, logical, and fair under the circumstances. In the emergency housing camp of Noisy-le-Grand, he established an association with the families. He restored the freedom of association, the freedom of thought and of speech. As early as 1957, without calling it by its real name yet, Father Joseph committed himself with the families to a struggle for human rights. By creating the "Group for Action, Culture, and Rehousing of Parisian Area Citizens," soon joined by the "European Brotherhood of Builders," he entrusted families from whom no one expected any good with the outcome of his own life as a man and a priest. Society took no notice. People in the immediate vicinity at best shrugged their shoulders. However, the Ministry of the Interior distrusted these developments.

*Father Joseph in his office in Noisy-le-Grand, 1964.*

"Very soon I realized that we could not achieve anything alone. The association had hardly been set up when I was summoned to police headquarters to give an explanation. Among the members of our Executive Committee were former convicts who had done time in prison. What kind of plot was I hatching here — an organization of criminals? I turned to a Protestant friend of mine, and we founded a new association. My friend requested that it be called "Aide A Toute Détresse."[8] That is how we lost a name that stood for something important to the families; but they agreed, since it did not change our aims."

Was not the essential point that the families themselves were the founders? Father Joseph would always refuse to claim any personal credit from this initiative. Yet was taking the very poor both as his first associates and as genuine partners not a tall order? "What else could I do? Don't imagine that I was pioneering in the field of participation. I was one of them; I belonged to their community. Like them, I was cold and hungry. They made fun of me because I was not taking advantage of my position as a priest. With whom else could I have formed an alliance? I shared an unbearable situation with the families. Had it lasted six months it would have been bearable; after a year, it would no longer have been. At the end of two years, the only alternative would have been rebellion or sinking to the bottom with the population. Our first organization arose out of a fear of this; it was a way of sharing the daily tragedy. Indeed, all that followed arose in the same way — from reality, from an excess of injustice, and from the fear of hitting the bottom together. Everything grew from a shared experience, never from a theory."

So fear continued to go hand in hand with trust in one's most humiliated brothers and sisters, with confidence in those who were the most diminished in the eyes of the world. For many years, the two would be inseparable. "How could trust exist without fear?" Father Joseph asks us with a smile. "Was it perhaps a way of the cross? In any event, it was our golden opportunity."

---

8 Aide A Toute Détresse ("Help to Every Distress") was the name given to this first organization which, thanks to constant growth and change, would become the International Movement ATD Fourth World.

# Chapter Nine

# "LET MY PEOPLE GO!"

## The Poor, Our Masters

Today, many of us carry memories in our hearts of Father Joseph as he was in 1959, "fully a priest in church, and a passionate fighter everywhere else." From that year on, we would be more and more numerous — families, friends, first Volunteers — to have met, and loved and followed him. What kept us from leaving him, what changed us profoundly has already come to light all along in these pages.

We met a man who had made a clear choice for a people that was in rags, deprived of all power, recognition, and prestige. Here was a man who did not make lengthy speeches about this choice, but who lived it right under our eyes, even accepting that the families' bad reputation cast a shadow over him as a priest. "If he's staying with them," people would say, "he can't be any better than they are." Frail as he was, living among his own, where did he find the determination, day after day, to face the opposition and interference that were preventing families from fleeing this hell? "Let my people go!" It was becoming clear that he had decided to lead these families out of darkness at a time when people everywhere were setting up roadblocks at the exits, especially in the direction of decent housing.

The local and national authorities wanted to get rid of what some described as a gangrene. ("They were ready to offer me important funding if I took this entire population away to an isolated spot in some remote part of the country.") Father Joseph paid no attention. There were 252 Quonset huts sheltering a number of households that were hard to count because some families offered temporary lodgings to others. There were at least a thousand children whose parents "were tossing and turning in the midst of terrible poverty as if they were trapped in a cage. I had soon realized that if we did not build together, even without resources, we were going to sink to the bottom." First, Father Joseph did what no one could stop him from doing: he built a chapel and organized catechism classes. "This is what I am qualified to do, and this is why my bishop sent me. How could you even think of preventing me from bringing God to them?" On Christmas Eve, when the ground was either frozen or sticky with mud, the table for supper after midnight mass was set for all. "Nothing was missing," Mrs. Aubert observed; and bystanders wondered, "How did this priest manage; isn't he overdoing things? They had cake, turkey, and champagne!" Mrs. Aubert added a subtle note: "There was always something special in the air: praying, celebrating the Child about to be born, as well as worrying about their own children and the new year, one more year to be spent in the Quonset huts."

*The chapel of the Camp of Noisy-le-Grand, built by Father Joseph in 1957.*

*The interior of the chapel. Stained glass windows by Jean Bazaine. "Nothing is too beautiful for the poor."*

On Good Friday, the Stations of the Cross also took on their full meaning once again in the narrow paths of the Camp in Noisy-le-Grand. Here too, onlookers wondered. "This just isn't done any more; why is he trying to bring back old traditions?"

Families living in the Camp had their own opinion about this event, which Charles Sleeth, one of the early Volunteers and an

American Protestant, describes as follows: "On Good Friday, I decided to follow a Stations of the Cross procession led by Father Joseph. As it went through the center of the shantytown, it elicited everyone's active participation. A large, noisy crowd, made up of adults, children, and dogs flowed together spontaneously. In the middle of the commotion, Father Joseph introduced the families as actors, having them read the texts at every station. He would exchange directly with them about everyday events in which they had played a part shortly before Easter. At the station where Veronica wipes Christ's face with a cloth, he said to a mother who was elbowing her way through the crowd, 'You see, it's like you when you forgive your husband who's beaten you, and when you make a fresh start in life with him.' All of this was happening in the midst of the bustle of shouting, barking, shoving, and incipient fighting that must have surrounded people's processions in other eras, but I clearly noticed that the families were deeply moved. The path Jesus took toward Golgotha was their path. How could anyone fail to be touched by this priest's genuine communion with these men and women whom he knew and loved so outstandingly and whom he called, by the strength of his faith, to self-sacrifice and to greatness. On the way home to go to bed, I felt that I had experienced a foretaste of resurrection."

In 1962, after a Stations of the Cross that ended in the midst of dust and of children shouting, Father Joseph repeated in the chapel these words of Saint Vincent de Paul, from which the young Volunteer Corps would draw its motto: "The poor are our masters; they remind us that Jesus is still stumbling past our doors on his way to Golgotha."

"The poor, our masters ..." Saint Vincent's words were going to acquire a new meaning during these years of living together in the Camp of Noisy-le-Grand. Father Joseph was going to give them their full scope. In his person, they were going to become an appeal to all human beings, rich and poor alike, without any cultural or religious distinctions. However, the very poor are no longer only masters to serve. They are masters who can teach us a new way of thinking. "The poor have an experience, and a way of thinking. Whether we are their neighbors in a run-down housing development or we are living in remote residential neighborhoods, they have unique knowledge to teach us about humanity, love, justice, and sharing. This remains true even if, through lack of education, their thinking is not well organized, their vocabulary is limited, and their speech hesitant."

During these years, Father Joseph often reminded us that, in the area of commitment to the poorest, we were not innovators but rather heirs. Saint Vincent wrote, "I should not look at a poor peasant or a poor woman according to their outer appearances, nor according to what seems to be the extent of their intelligence, all the more so since often they hardly look or act like reasonable people, coarse and earthy as they are. Yet look at the other side of the coin and you'll see through the eyes of faith that the Son of God, who wanted to be poor, is represented to us by these poor people." Have we always known how to interpret these words? For Christians, the very poor are not merely a symbolic image of the Lord. In the Camp of Noisy-le-Grand, Father Joseph taught the families and the first Volunteers that each human being was a person who should be loved by his fellow human beings whatever their beliefs might be. "It is very hard, even and especially for neighbors, to love the very poor since they are so disfigured. Yet the very way we look at them determines whether they will dare to hold their heads up high and to discover themselves transfigured, empowered, and intelligent. What do ideologies matter to us, as long as the most desperately broken families see in us a reflection of their own humanity? This humanity is neither an idea nor a legend; it does exist. For centuries, the very poor have expressed this to us. When they insult us in our welfare hotels, in our shelters, or at the entrances of our churches, they are taking revenge for not being loved for their own sakes as brothers and sisters." Did Saint Paul not say, "The particular way in which the Spirit is given to each person is for a good purpose"? [I Corinthians 12, v. 7-8] In Father Joseph's opinion, this statement applies to everyone, beginning with those who have been most humiliated, and each of us is responsible for enabling all human beings to show this gift which *is* in them.

If Father Joseph had envisioned priesthood in a different way, would the emergency housing camp have become the starting point of a movement in the 1960s? Ever since his days in Tergnier and in Dhuizel, it was obvious that, for him, being a priest meant that none of his fellow human beings' suffering could leave him untouched. "Loving people means wanting them to be free and able to accomplish more than we have accomplished. If we carry our beliefs as priests to their logical conclusion, this will lead us, sooner or later, into the area of citizenship and this is where society is waiting for us." Society was not always waiting with open arms.

As early as 1958, the soup kitchen closed down. "Men and women, carrying tin pots of donated food, used to walk all around the outer limits of the Camp to avoid passing by my shack, such was their shame and their awareness of the shame I felt for them. 'It's for my dog,' they said if they happened to meet me anyway. All these forms of assistance were only so many ways of giving up on the families, of imprisoning them in this Camp of suffering. They only added a little more every day to the poverty and humiliation of the families. This had prompted my decision to set up an association with people living in the Camp. Whatever the cost, we had to manage to keep only the essential and worthwhile services on the site. We had to be able to get rid of the invaders."

## A Library Instead of a Soup Kitchen, a Preschool Instead of Foster Care

What exactly were the essential services? The families themselves would make it clear. Thanks to Father Joseph's leadership, the soup kitchen was replaced by a library, even though the families living in the Quonset huts might have wanted electricity first. Gift packages from adoptive parents in the United States became rare. A preschool opened its doors. Handouts of used clothes were turned into a clothing thrift shop, and during the winter of 1959-60, unemployed fathers built the walls of a community center for women, as well as a modern laundromat. These were followed by a center for men and youths and a sub-contracting workshop that provided women and teen-age girls with work. Vacation camps for children were a highlight of the summer months, which were virtually unbearable in the Quonset huts. These camps put an end to the "holidays" that consisted of taking children away to stay with affluent Swiss or Belgian families for indefinite lengths of time. Such "holidays" meant that parents lost all control over their own children's future. The school attendance rate climbed from 60% to 90% between 1958 and 1965. All these projects were like stepping stones that continued the struggle to rehouse every family in a yet-to-be-built housing project for family advancement. Above all, there was the presence, day and night, of "Father Joseph, who knows each of us personally. To him, we are somebody; no one is like anyone else. The bottom line is that Father Joseph has made a somebody of each of us." Did this mean that Mr. Lefaou, who had already been living in the Camp for eighteen months before Father Joseph's arrival, had been a nobody? He was appreciated by many people since, at age sixty, he knew a lot about delivering babies, and, at the request of the Companions of Emmaus, he went the rounds as a town crier, announcing important news to the Camp's inhabitants. "But with Father Joseph, nothing was as before. We could tell him our point of view. I used to discuss business with him, and he would listen to me. He gave us back our honor."

*The laundry room in the Camp of Noisy-le-Grand, 1963.*

## Culture as a Weapon Against Extreme Poverty; but Who Will Get Top Priority?

Between 1957 and 1970, Father Joseph led a difficult struggle to rehouse the families, and, even beyond this, to obtain the right to decent housing for every family. On this front, he would win two battles: the construction of two housing projects for family advancement, and the rehousing of all the families living in the Camp. At the same time, in the background, another struggle was being waged. In fact, Father Joseph was fighting inch by inch against discouragement and shame, against a 'What's the use?' attitude, and for each and every person's honor. He was fighting for the right to culture. It was the very dream of Robert Garric[9] and his former social teams that reached a stunning fulfillment they had not dared to hope for themselves: a cultural center, a library, and the introduction of works of art, such as a bell tower, a wall that reflected rays of the sun rising over the kindergarten, and original paintings by Bazaine, Miro, and Chagall displayed on the walls of the women's community center. Jean Bazaine's stained-glass windows turned the igloo-shaped chapel into a radiant place for praying and meditating on God's words with hope, showing how Father Joseph always carried ideals to their fullest expression. What counted for Mr. Lefaou and for all the families was this struggle for the right to culture and spirituality and, ultimately, for the eminent dignity of human beings. "What purpose would the association have served if we had just let ourselves go?" asked Mrs. Parmentier, whose husband had been out of work for six years.

One might well wonder just why all these developments disturbed society the way they did. Maybe if Father Joseph had been a man managing on his own and staying put in just one place, maybe if he had just been an efficient grass-roots worker, might he have been less upsetting to his fellow citizens? No doubt, this is an academic question. For his ordination, Father Joseph had chosen this motto: "Put out into deep water and pay out your nets for a catch." "Pay out your nets" with what message? What kind of nets are these in which people are going to be gathered and which seem to have caused so much commotion?

Ever since he arrived in the Camp of Noisy-le-Grand, Father Joseph's very personality and way of life conveyed a question that, over the centuries, has confronted mankind with a lot of loose ends. If every person truly is a human being, then should not the most abandoned and despised be the first ones to be loved and reestablished in justice? Should they not always be our top priority? Without them, do human rights exist? Are all our struggles not unfair unless the very poor are our first partners? It is their priority in all our communities, our organizations, and our projects

9 Robert Garric was a popular educator of the masses in France. He recruited and trained teams of collaborators whose goal was to give the working poor access to all forms of culture as well as opportunities to express their love for and appreciation of culture.

that is at stake and that, in many people's opinions, turns society upside down. What are our endeavors worth if we do not give first place to the rejected?

"But partnership with the poorest" — Father Joseph will wonder all his life — "will the world ever want it?"

## Chapter Ten

# DIVE TO THE BOTTOM OR PUT OUT INTO DEEP WATER?

### The Birth of a Movement Struggling Upstream

Let us go back for a moment to the events of 1957: three hundred families, confined to a stretch of wasteland so that they would not have to display their wretchedness in front of everyone, joined forces around a priest in an association. Its name was "Group for Action, Culture, and Rehousing." Its goals were "to break free from isolation, to create resources for better living conditions, to build facilities for cultural expression, to lay the groundwork for solidarity with surrounding society and, thereby, to provide a people with a recognized identity and enable it to assume its rightful place in the history and in the future of mankind." "That was quite a program," Father Joseph would say in 1982, as if to apologize. "But it was, after all, what we were doing. We had not yet realized it, but we were setting up an international organization for the defense of human rights."

"Very soon, I realized that we could not achieve anything alone. We opened a bank account and appointed an accountant, Mrs. Fouchet, a mother from the Camp. I started to send out appeals for funds. They conveyed the suffering and the dignity of the families. They had a real impact and helped to make public opinion aware of the persistence of deepest poverty. Thus a movement of support arose that reached out to public opinion." These few words indicate the growth of the association, which became instrumental in starting the first projects in the Camp: water pumps, cement floors in the Igloo huts, a multipurpose-purpose community center, and summer camps. But this association of ordinary citizens was going to gain momentum. Father Joseph's appeals, just a few mimeographed sheets, soon became a small newsletter and then a monthly magazine: *Igloos*. Between 1960 and 1985, this publication would bear witness to rather unexpected growth. The small association was coming out of its cocoon. From a handful of families who had not managed to ingratiate themselves with the Ministry of the Interior sprang up a real movement of thinking and of action. The Movement was going to be based on a Volunteer Corps and would bring together members from every country, culture, and spiritual background. It would obtain consultative status with major European and United Nations' authorities. Families trapped in chronic poverty from four continents occupied center stage.

One thing remains obvious: "Everything arose from reality, from shared experience, never from a theory." The *Igloo* magazine, which portrayed the realities of poverty and which would soon be reinforced by conferences and seminars, gave rise to solid support but also to stubborn opposition. No doubt the confrontation during the 1960s with such harsh realities as "Children are dying from cold," and "Tuberculosis is still eating away at families," helped to build friendships. At the same time, it also triggered disbelief, irritation, and disagreement. These reactions would represent a burden, sometimes even a nightmare. Now, the refusal to recognize extreme poverty as a violation of human rights, the refusal to respect the victims' dignity, often resulted in real insults directed at the families by the mass media and public authorities. These reactions would delay legislative measures for a long time. For how could anyone redress a situation that public opinion refused to call by its true name? How could a human rights policy be developed on behalf of a population group that its fellow citizens described as families who are unstable, lacking will power, or even mentally retarded?

Public authorities cannot necessarily be blamed for this delay. A whole intellectual élite was going to great lengths to explain that Father Joseph's outlook was misguided. He was imagining poor people who did not really exist. Sociology and psychology were ready to prove what society had been saying about the very poorest for centuries: these families are not poor but rather maladjusted, misfits, marginal, emotionally disturbed, or problem families that we must educate. “Society had stripped them of all possessions to the point of depriving them of this ultimate right to be recognized as poor people.” Father Joseph wondered, “What have they got left now to defend themselves with?” Anyway, the Ministry of Public Health sent a psychiatrist and a sociologist as delegates to the Camp of Noisy-le-Grand to clarify matters.

## Scientific Research in Defense of the Honor of the Very Poor

Father Joseph, hurt by the humiliation heaped on these families, has already opened a small research office in the hope of setting reliable researchers into motion. From 1961 on, he will patiently surround himself with research workers who will discover and relate many things about chronic poverty that he, himself, has known since childhood. At his request, symposiums about poverty are organized at UNESCO headquarters in 1961 and 1964. He will lead the study groups created as a follow-up, which meet in Paris between 1962 and 1967. In 1964, he also founds an international research group on poverty within the IAS (International Association of Sociology). French as well as Belgian, British, Danish, Norwegian, and American sociologists and economists participate. At the opening of their first session, he is not afraid to assert, “The poorest of the poor are bearing the burden of the world’s ignorance. It weighs down on them like a slab of cement each time they try to lift up their heads.”

So the man of action made for wide-open spaces spends precious time in places of study so that knowledge may advance in a Europe that seems to have completely forgotten about poverty. The Movement, which would soon change its name from Aide A Toute Détresse to ATD Fourth World, would be the first non-governmental, anti-poverty organization to have its own Research Institute. Neither the man who founded it, nor the Volunteers who take charge of it, will avoid criticism: “They are using the poor as guinea pigs for their research work.” This will not prevent research about poverty from gaining momentum in Europe, thanks to this priest who visited university campuses in a threadbare cassock.

As for the Movement, it grew at the same pace as the heated discussions it aroused. In 1961, a delegation of families came from the shantytown of La Campa in the suburban town of La Courneuve. "Father, we are being tracked down. You are the only one who can do anything." In 1965, the City of Paris asked the organization to send some of its members to La Cerisaie, an emergency housing project in the suburban town of Stains. Other emergency housing developments such as les Emouleuses in Créteil, and les Grands Chênes in Versailles were waiting too. Other people were waiting for Volunteers — and this came as a surprise — in the Lower East Side of New York, the Frimhurst Family Center in Great Britain, the Heuvelkwartier of Breda in the Netherlands, downtown Luxembourg, Fribourg in Switzerland, the Molenbeek neighborhood in Brussels, and the disused army barracks overcrowded with low-income families in Rastatt, West Germany. Soon the Movement was attracting men and women from every continent. As early as 1965, Father Joseph was being asked for in India.

*Extreme poverty crosses all boundaries. Father Joseph with the author traveling to Cologne to visit emergency housing shelters for the homeless and to make new friends. Paris, 1961.*

In Western Europe and in industrialized countries generally, the vision that inspired Father Joseph in 1957 proves to be true throughout these formative years. We are indeed dealing with a people that shares a common history: that of the excluded, which is the same across national borders. And this people has its own common memory, life styles and ways of thinking, as well as its own unique bonds of kinship. We have come a long way since the solitary confinement of families in the Camp of Noisy-le-Grand; these families have discovered that they belong to a vast population group they no longer have to be ashamed of. Step by step with the help of the Volunteer Corps, these families piece together their history. They also uncover the history of what used to be called the "Fourth Estate" or "Fourth Order," when, on the eve of the French Revolution, the very poor were considered unworthy of political representation. "We are the Fourth World," they are now saying with pride.

During their annual meeting in 1973, Fourth World youths were amazed. "We have a history of our own. This is fantastic! Father Joseph says so, and he is right." Indeed, Father Joseph could not be misled either about the "new poor" whom affluent countries imagined they were discovering in the 1970s, or about people who had always been poor. He was a witness to the persistence of extreme poverty of families from the Saint-Nicolas neighborhood whom he knew during his childhood; of families from Saint-Crépin or Saint-Médard, whom he visited as a seminarian in Soissons; as well as of families from the Moulin Neuf housing project in Stains whom he knew in the 1970s. It was because the history of the very poor had been taken from them and thrown away, and to ensure that this could no longer happen, that Fourth World Volunteers would become their chroniclers. Father Joseph had initiated daily observation reports as a way for Volunteers to reconsider the meaning of their lives and to guarantee each Volunteer's communion with the suffering and hopes of the very poor. As Father Joseph said, "The observation report is like a prayer that unites us beyond our religious beliefs." At his request, it also became a way to pay special attention to people's history, a way to restore to all of them a sense of their roots, their identity and their dignity as participants in the history of mankind.

When families who had felt so ashamed about their past really understood this, they began to look for, to write or to dictate material themselves. This happened around 1968. Only then did we see that the anxiety that had filled Father Joseph since his arrival in the Camp of Noisy-le-Grand began to subside. This suffering on the families' behalf never let go of him. It always remained alive within him right beside trust, optimism, and good humor. It brought forth those outbursts of anger which, like thunderstorms, would sweep an overcast sky clear. While relieving everyone, they restored people's sense of modesty as well as their fighting spirit. Still, thanks to this commitment to writing, the anxiety he felt about the families' weaknesses did lose a little of its sting. "Whoever has come to terms with his past and takes pride in his elders' determination to go on living is ready to become a defender of his people, an agent not only for his own rights but also for human rights generally."

## Human Rights and Political Representation

The turning point came in 1968. The crucial events of the spring[10] hastened its arrival, but it would have happened anyway. Father Joseph was not merely developing a program of grass-roots activities with families from poverty-stricken areas. He was leading a history forward with his people, and he urged them on just as he urged on everyone within reach, including God, to ensure that this history march on to the goal set eleven years earlier in a camp sunk in mud. This apparently conventional progress toward a slightly better life was being made by means of unpretentious projects, such as a preschool for young children, clubs and travel for young people, and meetings among parents. Yet who around Father Joseph could be unaware that all of this fitted together within the context of a history that was anything but commonplace? This same history was going "to provide a people with a recognized identity and enable it to assume its rightful place in the history and in the future of mankind." Public authorities were probably not expecting this kind of project or this way of talking. To those who were close to Father Joseph, they seemed to become not only conceivable, but even self-evident. How could anyone not want universal brotherhood and complete justice after they had been confronted with what Father Joseph, right up to his very last days, denounced as overwhelming inhumanity, overwhelming injustice, and overwhelming suffering? In any case, families trapped in relentless poverty were aware of this, even if they found only a few words to say so: "He gives us back our dignity," or, "With him, honor is back in our lives," or "With him, we will manage to have everyone getting along together."

In France, at any rate, the events of 1968 threw the Movement head over heels into the future that Father Joseph was expecting. Because of national strikes, it was first of all a time of increased deprivation and humiliation. No more entitlement checks, no more

---

10 The crucial events of the spring of 1968 were widespread national strikes throughout France, triggered by violent student protests and revolts in most French universities. The longer these strikes lasted, the more they paralyzed everyday life, causing serious shortages of food and fuel and very long delays in their distribution.

work at even the lowest-paid bread-winning job, no more medical care and no more relatives or neighbors available to help. A whole people at the foot of the social ladder was threatened by starvation for the sake of a struggle that was not their business and that no one asked them to join. Disturbing times, indeed, when some of the Volunteers took to the streets of Paris to collect money so that children would not die of hunger, while others, taking their cue from the history of the revolution of 1789, went from one poverty-stricken area to another to encourage inhabitants to write down their grievances in so-called "Cahiers de Doléances."[11] In Father Joseph's opinion, now was the time to change defeat into victory. With the money and food supplies given by concerned citizens, he, too, went from one housing project to another. "You have to form committees," he would say. "You are going to do by yourselves what other people have been doing for you as a matter of course for ages. You are going to distribute money and food, but in a fair way, by giving help first to those who need it the most." To a population group filled with anguish because it had never learned how to handle such distributions and who shunned this responsibility, he declared, "It is going to be now or never. Aren't you citizens too?"

As early as the month of May, Father Joseph launched "Learning in the Streets" with students on strike. This experience of "sharing knowledge" would later spread to areas of extreme poverty on four continents. On July 14, 1968, in la Cerisaie, the most abandoned housing project in the Parisian area, these students staged a play about the French Revolution with the inhabitants. The nation's capital paid no attention, but the poorest among the poor began to ease their way into French society and to "assume their rightful place in the history of mankind." Their struggle finally took on the

11 Cahiers de Doléances (Redress Notebooks) were begun by a noble, Dufourny de Villiers, to record testimonies from poor peasants and workers at the height of the French Revolution. One day Father Joseph was looking through old books in a Paris bookstore, and he came across a completely forgotten work written by Dufourny de Villiers in 1979, entitled *Notebooks of the Fourth Order, the One that Includes Poor Day Laborers, the Disabled, Paupers, etc. The Holy Order of Unfortunate People*. Father Joseph coined the expression "Fourth World" in reference to this "Fourth Order," which had been excluded from society.

name of a struggle for human rights. From then on, the door was open to genuine representation of the Fourth World wherever other citizens were discussing and making decisions about the future.

## With the Poorest, No Death Without Resurrection

Father Joseph had been taking responsibility for representation ever since 1957, in fact. We have only just begun to understand how he was able to remain faithful to his ideal of totally immersing himself among the poorest while setting out into the world, "paying out his nets into deep water." How did he manage to be more than merely available, sharing with his whole being in the anxieties, the catastrophes, and the rays of hope of the most rejected? Mrs. Aubert recalls the early years. "He would never go anywhere unless someone had asked him to come. But whenever a crisis broke out, he was always there, often late at night. Then he used to stay with them all night if he had to. He would never leave before he had reestablished peace. Still," she adds, " there was no end to it. There were always families who were even more wretched than the others. And new ones kept arriving, too." How many meals did he share together around a family table, how many parties, marriages, and baptisms were celebrated together, how much time was spent with children? (Was there even one child who did not share his secrets with him?) How much patient presence and tenderness he showed in the art of taking time with people as if nothing was calling him elsewhere!

How did he manage to stay motionless for hours by the side of a woman who had been abandoned by her husband and who had run out of hope? How did he manage at the same time to lead the public struggle in Paris and in the government's ministries, blazing a trail both through the offices and through the confusion prevailing in ideas about extreme poverty? He traveled to give homilies and lectures throughout France. Where did he, who had been plagued by fear and shyness, find not only the time but also the conviction and the confidence to do all this?

"My brother, discouraged? Never!" Louis Wresinski is astounded that anyone could even ask. "The other day, he came in with a bloodstained cassock. There had been a fight, I suppose, but he had things to do in Paris. So he stopped by our house to wash up. My brother is not the kind of person who gets discouraged." Father Joseph was even more emphatic himself. "Total immersion on the one hand, and putting out into deep water on the other, are less contradictory than one might think. I really plunged deeply into the misery of Noisy-le-Grand, and I asked the first Volunteers to go just as far. Yet the fact that I really wanted to bury myself in the midst of such an impoverished population group, the fact that I tried to carry out this approach completely, led me to understand that there was no way of dying with the very poor unless it became a way of rising with them too. The very poor themselves must become messengers in humanity... Sinking down into an environment of desolation, with no resources and no way to defend myself, forced me to go farther than ever 'into deep water.' I have always felt that this was our good fortune."

As for trust, Mrs. Jacques, seated on the only chair left in her unheated Quonset hut, explains to us, "Father Joseph does not ***believe*** in God. That is what my husband says. Father Joseph ***knows*** God ***intimately***; he speaks with Him; he knows. At mass, he scolds us for not acting like Him. 'If you talked to God more often, he would stop at nothing to get you out of this mess.'" A Parisian friend who often visited the chapel adds, "Father Joseph speaks to God like the Israelites used to in the Old Testament. He asks God what He is waiting for to set his people free."

Without this trust, would Father Joseph perhaps have become a manager or even an activist? He had his way of being both fully a priest and fully a responsible citizen, without ever sacrificing one to the other. "He was a priest in everything that he did," said Jean Theisen, a Volunteer from Luxembourg. "But he knew how to be one in all things without ever alienating those who did not hold the same beliefs as his. That was his secret."

Plunging into the heart of the very poor so as to put out all the better into deep water, putting out into deep water so as to gather men and women around the very poor: shaping a world that believed in this would require the creation of a Volunteer Corps.

# Chapter Eleven

# IT IS TIME TO INVEST PEOPLE IN PEOPLE AGAIN

### "A Volunteer Corps Wanting What We Wanted: To End Extreme Poverty"

When he spoke about the way he began in the Camp of Noisy-le-Grand, Father Joseph stated, "The idea of a *Volontariat*[12] followed almost immediately, and without this *Volontariat* arising out of the wretchedness of the Camp, nothing could have been achieved. What could the families and I do if men and women wanting to end extreme poverty, just as we did, had not come forward to join us? I felt the absolute necessity for Volunteers devoted to the poorest, but I still had no clear idea of such a Volunteer Corps in my mind."

As he watched Father Joseph develop projects, a movement, and a Volunteer Corps, a friend wrote to us in the 1960s, "His resources are so scarce and still he sets out to do the job and he moves ahead. No doubt, his motto is, 'The Lord helps those who help themselves.'" This was not altogether accurate. Father Joseph never started his projects just by relying on God's grace. He did not get ahead of God. In his opinion, God was in the forefront, leading a history with His people. "Only God is always on time," he wrote in his journal in 1959. We find this other statement there too: "There are no great men; there is God." Yet another example:

12 The Volontariat is the French term for the International Volunteer Corps. Teams of volunteers were set up in various countries in Europe in the 1960s, in the United States in 1964, then in Canada in 1979, in Asia, Latin America, and Africa. There are now some 350 full-time volunteers, representing many different cultures, creeds, and professions, working in 23 countries on five continents.

an do no harm to God. By insulting God, we can only bring His mercy. We cannot hurt him. The only way we can affect is through human beings, by harming the poor who are not only His children but also His Son... God wants each family to be happy; our task is to actually create happiness." Even while living among the very poor without any resources himself, he wrote in 1959, "If you are not thinking about God every minute, if you are not constantly working in union with God, then what's the good of being alive?"

For Father Joseph, therefore, the idea was not to follow his own agenda, but rather to take part in a clearly drawn history. Fourth World families have their own history. Unfortunately for them, others have too often interfered in it in a destructive way. People are constantly meddling with it according to their goodwill, their ignorance, or their repulsions. Yet when they go too far, they cause history to take its revenge. When the very poor are confined in housing projects rife with injustice, the scandal is bound to break out into the open some day. What matters is that those who share in these families' lives look with modesty and lucidity for the role they should play, the effort they should make, and the kind of person they should be in the struggle of the very poor. Father Joseph called on the first Volunteers to join in this quest.

*Mass on Christmas Eve in La Campa, 1968. "And it came to pass, in those days, that people decided to destroy shantytowns. They held a census of all the wretched of the earth who happened to be in shantytowns and rough-and-ready housing projects."*

He did not do so because short-term volunteering was fashionable in this post-war era. An entire generation of European youths, it is true, was crossing borders in those days to devote a time of service to population groups in trouble. These young people came to the Camp, just as they would go to other places. But their presence did not change the families' state of dependency. Rather it emphasized the overall incoherence, the lack of control the families could have over their own lives. Once again, Father Joseph could not put up with blind generosity over which families have no influence or control. "It is unthinkable that we send into shantytowns... people who have no training at all, who lack sufficient knowledge because they have neither a profession nor maturity to draw on. True charity would consist in training experienced and skilled people to serve the poor. It is only when it fulfills this requirement that society is entitled to introduce itself in their midst." In the Camp of Noisy-le-Grand, among his own people, Father Joseph charted another course to follow for men and women from all backgrounds and of all ages. He fostered another kind of commitment, a commitment not for people of goodwill but rather for people with willpower, "wanting what we wanted: to end extreme poverty." Such a commitment had to be created and, here again, everything had to start with the realities of a life genuinely shared with the families.

"No doubt I did call them, but they had to fashion their lives on their own. I was not one of them; I did not come from where most of them came. They answered my call, but they had to shape their lives and personalities on their own."

## The First Volunteers: "It Made Our Hearts Ache to Share the Same Suffering"

Volunteers do not feel that they have shaped themselves on their own. Did Father Joseph not mould them one by one as he did the families of the Camp? Did he not devote to them his boundless patience, indulgence, and tenderness to help them grow? He most certainly did. Everyone concerned will say so and write about it over the years; and, after his return to God, personal accounts abound.

"First, Father Joseph was really hoping that I would become a good psychologist. This was a bottom line on which he placed all his other expectations. For twelve years, at each of our meetings, he reminded me, 'Debuyst always said that you were going to become a good psychologist.' He had a dream for me as well as for all the other Volunteers. Then he was hoping that I would take my place fully within the Volunteer Corps and that I would experience the joy of making my own personal contribution. He was looking for this place with me; he was concerned about it."

"He stripped us to the bone. With him, all our theories were pulverized in front of the question: Do you love your neighbor; do you love the poorest of the poor? Even though we were all so different, he still knew how to make each of us understand what mattered in life."

"Father Joseph did not ask me to be a Volunteer. Merely by the things he suggested I could do, he made me take the right direction. He knew I was afraid, even without my telling him so. He trusted people; he allowed me to take one step at a time. I thought I was leading an interesting life. The life he opened up before me was so much more genuine and important. When I think of this remote Camp steeped in mud beyond every road and street, it makes me wonder: How did he manage to make me believe in something truly great?"

"Father Joseph was ill. Although he was exhausted and had barely recovered, he insisted on coming to Nancy. The first part of that visit took place in the hospital room where Jean-Pierre Bertran was clinging to life, with his eyes his only means of communication. Deeply moved as he stood next to the man who had been the first Volunteer in Nancy, Father Joseph merely said, 'Thank you, thank you...' He took a long look at him; he stayed a long time. Here was a man and a priest who not only was living according to the Gospel, but whose acts and thoughtfulness were also a direct expression of God's love. He let God's love shine through him... But this is what I believe; it is not right for me to impose this on the whole Volunteer Corps."

Father Joseph and the Volunteers... there would be so much more to tell. They will recount it in other books. True, he was not one of them. He reminded them of this. "I am a priest and a man coming from extreme poverty." His main concern was to respect them as persons coming from other backgrounds. He offered them room where they could shape their lives freely. That explains why this Volunteer Corps, springing up in the Camp of Noisy-le-Grand, had no rules, but only some basic guidelines developed, little by little, through life, misfortune, and the expectations of the families.

Between Father Joseph, these first Volunteers and the families, a story was being enacted then — one we recognize today as a story of love. "It made our hearts ache to share the same suffering — that of being unable to remove so much chronic poverty all at once, that of enduring endless attacks and abuse." But who could tell in the 1960s whether trust or mistrust — the determination to end extreme poverty or the passionate longing to flee from it forever — would gain the upper hand? Perhaps trust of the same quality as Father Joseph's just had to win. For he acted with Volunteers as he did with families: he put his own fate into their hands.

If he had been looking for personal prestige, he would have acted completely differently with the families as well as with the Volunteer Corps. As a man who had clear goals in mind, he would have created an organization in no way dependent on the goodwill, the talents, the participation, and the unity of other people. But he wanted freedom and greatness for others. The families' freedom and greatness seemed to him to be inseparable from that of the Volunteers. So, at the very most, when faced with too much ignorance, awkwardness, or slowness on the part of Volunteers, he would sometimes issue a warning. "If you go on like this, I'll leave you and start a new movement with the families." It was his way of reminding us again that, in the presence of the very poorest people, Volunteers ought to strive to become responsible and free people. Their conduct and their rules — if these had to be codified some day — would not be dictated by him but rather by life shared together in the midst of deepest poverty. His own situation was too different; he knew he came from another background, and he could only patiently suggest ways of being and of doing things. He owed it to the families not to let Volunteers with a new way of presenting themselves turn into new oppressors. He was constantly keeping an eye on this, not without getting angry sometimes, but also with great humility. Accounts of meetings in the early 1960s bear witness to this. "I am just advancing some ideas; you will have to talk about them together," he would say; or, "This is only a suggestion. For all I know ..." Volunteers were free. Perhaps that made things even harder. But how could anyone not want to rise to the challenge of this founder who wanted them to be free and to surpass themselves?

During an interview in the 1980s, he evoked these first Volunteers with that confidence and tenderness that seem to have carried the day in the end. "The first team lived in Noisy-le-Grand, defenseless, empty-handed, deprived of everything, and having no answers to anything. They did not know where all of this would lead them. These first Volunteers, by the way, ought to continue guaranteeing the authenticity of this history today. The Volunteer Corps will have to stay this way: defenseless and always searching for which society, which democracy, which Church, which God... The day Volunteers believe that they have the answers, the very poor would no longer be able to express themselves; their message would be lost once more.

"Just imagine that a whole country was denying the existence of this population; a whole country was rejecting a valid solution. France and Europe were certainly not rejecting the idea of homelessness, but they were choosing the homeless who suited their fancy. Those whom we used to call the excluded were considered undesirable. Nothing was planned for them; and who, at that time, wanted to plan our institutions and our laws for them? Volunteers were being belittled by public authorities. 'Look at those ladies who are knitting again for the poor... Some of them over there are treating themselves to university studies at the expense of the families in the Camp.' We were being fought on all sides. Why did they stay? No doubt each one of them thought, 'I cannot turn my back on this misery, for it is destroying my brothers and sisters, and if it destroys them, it will destroy me.' They were the ones who refused to leave. The families did not yet know how to make them stay. They were accustomed to seeing people come and go. They were also suspicious; they were so used to having to sell their misery to get something in return. They had a hard time believing that someone could be unselfish. They were forced to take advantage of their extreme poverty themselves, so why should Volunteers not do so as well?

"Furthermore, these folks who were suggesting that the families shoulder their own responsibilities made it clear to them that they would have to pay a price to overcome their shame. We must understand the state of degradation caused by outbursts of public charity: Suchard Company trucks unloading chocolate bars, Swiss friends organizing endless vacations for children without even consulting their parents... Never has a population group been so stifled and so rejected by people claiming to assist it. These families could not help agreeing with us. They also could not help putting their hands over their ears and running away from us."

"The men and women who did stay were those who understood that the issue was not to find out who was to blame. They stayed to raise the real question, 'What is in the hearts and souls of these people living here, banished from the world and yet constantly threatened by it?' During those early years, Volunteers also experienced in their own hearts and souls the state of unending watchfulness, as well as the fear haunting families who knew that they were unwanted and never safe from ill-inspired interference. They accepted being insulted (as I myself was at times) by the very people whom they were trying to help. Our brother, this man, haunted by never-ending fear: 'Just have a look at me! Am **I** someone who could be lucky? With a face like mine, who could love me?' I believe that the first Volunteers lived in communion with this fear. In the Camp of Noisy-le-Grand, a communion sprang up between families and Volunteers, the likes of which I am not sure will be seen again. I then understood that they could form the Volunteer Corps the families needed if they could learn to live in communion with each other."

## He Shaped Them, One by One

Father Joseph would always talk this way about Volunteers, as if he, himself, had played no part in the calling that made them stay. Yet he never stopped helping that calling to grow stronger and become clearer. "A few years ago," he wrote to Francine de la Gorce[13] in 1968, "the issues were not put in those terms. We were simply ourselves in the presence of a group of families to be loved

[13] Francine de la Gorce, born in Belgium and currently Vice President of the Movement ATD Fourth World/France, was one of five women to set no limit to the length of time they would stay and work with very poor families in the Camp of Noisy-le-Grand. Thanks to training and encouragement from Father Joseph, this group of very early Volunteers coalesced into a loose, flexible prototype of the International Volunteer Corps.

and served. We had no time to ask ourselves questions about our difficulties and our inner contradictions... Have we understood clearly enough that we were not promoters of a revolution or a revolt, but rather advocates of a people? Serving a revolution requires only solidarity; serving a people requires communion. A people is not an ideal in and of itself. The ideal is this people's march forward, its justice, its freedom, everything that transcends it and enables it to advance. That requires of us idealism, communion, and commitment. Wanting commitment without communion is like wanting to go somewhere without taking the right road."

Thanks to Father Joseph, during those years of great fragility, Volunteers did at least learn to be in communion, in their own way, with the fragility both of the families and of the man who wanted to enable these families to emerge. This is how the history of Noisy-le-Grand became a love story. What kept them going in their awkward situation was the truth that shone through the life of the man who had called them. In his diocese, people had said that he was "a real priest." Volunteers holding different beliefs discovered a real human being, "who lives and talks according to what he thinks and what he believes in." In those days already, Father Joseph suggested that they meet together in annual sessions of a founders' conference (the "Assises"[14]). They were six, nine, fifteen... each year a few more, who took some days off, leaving helpers in charge, among whom, as "people always ready to walk the extra mile," the Volunteers were looked on as unbelievably idealistic. During their "Assises," they talked a lot about commitment to the families and less about the community among themselves that Father Joseph was longing for. From then on, while watching their slow and often painful headway, he would feel just as responsible for the Volunteers as for the families. He sensed, more strongly than they did themselves, their need to be helped to form a closely knit group. By the end of the 1960s, on the other hand, families had to rise to a new challenge — learning how to deal with a greater distance be-

14 "Assises" is the name Father Joseph gave to intensive sessions of meetings of Volunteers with at least five years of commitment. For the Assises, these Volunteers free themselves from their other tasks to examine and discuss together certain key questions about the nature and meaning of their own involvement with Fourth World families.

tween themselves and Father Joseph. That was how Father Joseph decided to leave the area in 1968, moving into a new place waiting to be built: a home base for the Volunteer Corps in Pierrelaye.

Once again, the man made for wide-open spaces put down roots in one spot. The man who could not stop crisscrossing countries around the world in search of his own would adhere again to a highly disciplined daily schedule: morning meetings; hours, days, and weeks of patient training of the Volunteers; endless personal correspondence; visits to the hospital or to Volunteers' parents, as well as close personal contacts with each and every one of them. One by one, he helped shape these Volunteers who, he would always say, forged their own identity. He was right inasmuch as he was always suggesting to them projects they felt went beyond their abilities. He let them find out for themselves what they were able to handle.

"It was much later that I understood that, as for Volunteers, Father Joseph always aimed farther than they thought they could go themselves," writes Annie van den Bosch, a Dutch Volunteer. Other Volunteers share her opinion:

"Above all, Father Joseph frightened me. He seemed to believe I was a lot stronger than I really was."

"Such an outlook, such trust, such love so far-reaching as to include so many people, all these people and even me... This can turn your life head over heels, and tenderness takes on real meaning."

"That day, he entrusted us with shooting a short film for a French television network. We thought they were either crazy or blissfully ignorant in that Movement. Tasks that overwhelmed us, as they had overwhelmed others before us, were beginning..."

"I was afraid of him. I was terrified by the trust he put in us. He quickly considered us team leaders. One day, I told Monique, 'But he's crazy to treat us like that. He does not know us; we have spent less time in the Movement than anyone else.' She replied: 'He knows you better than you think. He rarely makes mistakes. He knows he can trust you.' I was afraid of this trust; it did not feel comfortable."

"Perhaps I learned like a child because I felt loved, because I enjoyed a trust I could not betray."

Father Joseph often stepped in to sweep aside this extra load of seriousness and fear. "Above all, make sure that each time you meet the families, they will be able to say, 'We had a good laugh.' Come on, you're great! You're no fools."

By showing exemplary trust, he was also teaching them to trust others in turn, thereby training new generations of Volunteers. By taking part in each person's concerns and hopes, he became the reference point for the deep fellowship that he was expecting among Volunteers. He paid the price for it, just as he had paid the price for the truly common destiny he hoped for between Volunteers and Fourth World families. "If you do not succeed, I myself will have failed." He had agreed to pay this price for the families' whole-hearted participation; he agreed to pay it for the Volunteers' commitment. In his opinion, it was definitely one and the same community of common destiny: "If poor people do not find reference communities that prove to them that committing oneself is possible and that it can shape the world, they will never free themselves together. In that case, not one of them will be free."

## Learning from a People in Extreme Poverty

But what did committing oneself consist of? Father Joseph mistrusted the notion of "listening" that fascinated social workers in the 1960s and 1970s. In his opinion, people talked a lot about it, perhaps without always fully realizing what it was all about. "We are not just listening, we are learning; that is a different matter. We are learning from a people. And since its situation changes and it also moves forward, we can never predict in detail the kind of struggle the Volunteer Corps is going to carry out under its influence. If we are in communion with this population, something new will always result from this. Something original will inevitably come from it too, since our teacher is a people that has never yet been taken seriously.

"The Volunteer Corps is composed of people who think. But they do not merely repeat ready-made ideas, wrapped up in paper and tied with a ribbon. They represent an ongoing thinking process because they are in communion with human beings who are living, moving ahead, and thinking. The Volunteer Corps has ideas about love, peace, and justice, about all the world's major questions, but these ideas are never completely finished. Theirs is a true-to-life way of thinking, which is constantly confronted with the reality of people's lives, sorrows, and hopes. This new way of thinking cannot stand still. This, by the way, is what so unsettles those who are watching us. This mode of thought is not reassuring, since it prompts us really to devote our life and our personality to helping develop this reflection further. It may not be hard to create communities around a fully developed mode of thought. Our task is to build a community around an unfinished set of ideas that we must experience in unity with one another to carry it further."

And Father Joseph adds: "Last night, one of us tried to make a diagram: ways of thinking specific to the Movement, common and divergent ways of thinking among Volunteers. I am sure that all the sociologists, economists, and everyone who has majored in 'Political Sci.' would have found their heart's delight in all of that. But there it is! It is our good fortune that we can not behave this way at all. We are being moulded by learning from a people that is our teacher. Our only concern is to find out how we are going to allow ourselves to be taught and what we are going to learn from this teacher."

These comments go back to 1979. It has already taken ten years of perseverance to invent training that will lead to a Corps of Volunteers that meets the families' aspirations and is able to last. "This population is guiding us, but we are also guiding this population. During the early years, they mistrusted us, and they were right. Today they trust us wherever we are; are they still right? Are we sure that we know, not so much toward which society, but toward which way of being we are inviting them to move? If they take us seriously, where will they be going in their very inner being? They have been waiting forever for their freedom, but they have not been waiting to get their freedom from us. They have not asked us for anything. Year in and year out, Bernadette Cornuau[15] reminds us that the question is: in whose name, for the sake of what, do we claim to be fighting at these families' side?"

15 Bernadette Cornuau is another member of the group of five women who became the first Volunteers.

## A Community of Common Destiny

This was how Father Joseph spoke to us and explained things, meeting after meeting, from 'Assises' to 'Assises.' Still, could he have convinced people like us, who had been trained in quite different ways, if we had not seen him live what he believed in? Over the years, he himself became something of a living encyclopedia on chronic poverty in the world. Yet, he spent his time asking questions, consulting, and reading. Before every important step, before every decision involving the future, he went back to walk through a poverty-stricken housing project or to sit down with a family in a remote shack. "What do you say about that? In your opinion...? What would you do in my place?" In the evening, at home or during his travels, in a train, on a plane, he used to read for hours, line by line, the observation reports coming to him from teams on four continents. This was what he used to call "letting the people be judge and jury of everything". He would also consult Volunteers and interns, have his lectures and articles reread by others and rewrite them three times, six times, until late at night. "Because an idea is never finished, words will always be insufficient when they concern the very poor. Just imagine that they can neither protect themselves against us nor contradict us."

Experiencing, sustaining, and conceiving together this community of common destiny would remain Father Joseph's overriding concern until the very end. "Will they know how to build this kind of community?" He did not suggest any rules; he hoped for a growing awareness. "We are not people who commit ourselves merely as professionals, nor even as friends. We are putting our destiny on the line, knowing that we are affected by what affects our neighbor, changing ourselves in terms of what others need, at the risk of having to change our own ideas about life."

In January 1988, he still addresses a letter to the "Assises" Conference to be held in August, when Volunteers would no longer see him in their midst. "I would have liked to create communities of lay people whose members would live intimately linked, for and through one another, drawing their strength from the liberation of the very poor. I had thought that these communities would be a new way of living a faith, a hope, and a brotherhood because the poorest families would show us these three paths. The families should enable us every day of our lives to rewrite the sacred books and the writings of our masters in humanity so that they would truly become our masters. That would require of us a genuine reliance on the families, but also a commitment of each of us to the community of Volunteers. For this community is the crucible that enables us to find our way back into what is universal and to experience it, each of us, intensely according to our convictions. I imagined these communities turned toward the future, sensing through them the future of the families who, thanks to us, would disclose ever more clearly the true meaning of freedom, brotherhood, and justice. Linked to these small communities, which would belong to the overall community of Volunteers, these families would have been creators of a new world that all human beings carry within themselves, even if they have lost the key to it."

This is how Father Joseph patiently recalls once again what he expects from this Volunteer Corps while allowing it time to mature. He does not fail to add that he trusts these Volunteers, whose difficulties living as a united group put their honesty to the test every single day. "I have no doubt that some day a new form of community, of living together, based on the families and constantly striving to create the future, will emerge from the Volunteer Corps." What is essential is that we firmly continue our search together. This is what he will explain once again to young trainees.

"We are staking our lives on a people that is neither recognized nor wanted, that confers neither prestige nor security. In areas of extreme poverty, in the Fourth World, we are involved in a struggle that seems disreputable in the world's eyes. How can we claim to last unless we are united, unless we help one another? We are of all beliefs; we are not linked together as members of one particular religion. We are endeavoring to practice true charity and to share love. We are struggling against bottomless poverty according to the faith that is inside each of us. In order to be united, we must trust in one another's faith. We must make ourselves small so that our neighbor may grow in whatever he deeply believes in. Are we ready to search for what that means?"

Father Joseph never required Volunteers to understand everything, even less to let their commitment be dictated to them. He simply expected them to set out in the right direction. He knew that understanding would come with experience. Provided that they dared to follow the path toward community, it would lead them to a deeper understanding of this interfaith Volunteer Corps they were already forming. He could not go on with them long enough to see them reach this understanding. He just remained long enough to see them taking the right path. When he saw this, Father Joseph knew that he had been right in trusting that "there are no great men, there is God." After the 1970s, which he spent in exhausting efforts to forge unity and love among one and all, the 1980s would be a time of greater serenity. This was the moment when Father Joseph asserted, "It is time to invest people in people again." He said so during an evening gathering of United Nations officials in New York in 1985. With his deep concern for the very poor around the world, he would not have talked this way about the Volunteer Corps if he had been worried about its future.

"It is only today that, within the United Nations system, we are discovering human misery as a wound inflicted on human beings, a wound that undermines their faith in themselves, in those close to them, and in all people. We are discovering that families whose confidence has been undermined this way are unable to pass on any faith in life to their children. We are also discovering that, to get back on their feet again quickly, entire population groups today need others to come share their confidence and their lives. Today this kind of Volunteer Corps does exist: men and women who do not abandon a population after a short period of technical cooperation, but who commit themselves totally for many years."

## "They Are My Family"

From then on, Father Joseph would also speak with complete confidence about the Gospel account on the washing of the feet.[16]

[16] The washing of the feet, related in John, 13, 1-17, occurs while Jesus is instituting the last supper with his disciples. Jesus certainly intended to set an example for his disciples in the act of washing their feet, as he clearly stated, "You call me Master and Lord, and rightly; so I am. If I then, the Lord and Master, have washed your feet, you should wash each other's feet. I have given you an example so that you may copy what I have done to you.

I tell you most solemnly,
no servant is greater than his master,
no messenger is greater than the man who sent him.

Now that you know this, happiness will be yours if you behave accordingly."

It was as precious to him as the Gospel about the Temptation in the desert. Volunteers of all beliefs understand what he meant about the humility and help they owe one another. His confidence has won the day, and in his January 1988 editorial in the Movement's French-language newspaper, *Feuille de Route*, he expressed his joy. The man who remained all his life a man from extreme poverty said about Volunteers, "They are my family." He entrusted their basic security both to all the Movement's friends and to Fourth World families.

"They are my family..." These words will help his companions, who demanded so much of him, to bear the grief of his departure. Once again, he made them surpass themselves. In the 1960s, he said, "What would the families and I have become without them?" In 1988, "I recognize them as my own."

With Fourth World families as his native country and the Volunteer Corps as his family, how could Father Joseph not continue to teach a true community to us even today? His last tape recording, which he dictated at Foch Hospital the evening before his operation, accompanies us on our way toward the future. "We are committed to creating a spiritual climate, because the spirit must dwell in us. The spirit is a kind of awareness of the other person — a kind of communion with someone else so that, the weaker and smaller he is, the greater and more important he becomes to us.

"Speaking about spirituality leads us to the question of religion, of our relationship with God. We can call this the pinnacle of spirituality, its summit. However, we have to live a spirituality between people. This means a certain way of seeing people and of being with them. Just as we adopt an attitude of contemplation and of prayer with respect to God, trying to be silent and to draw as close as possible to Him, in the same way, we must be attuned to the spirituality of our brothers and sisters. We need to achieve a certain way of living with others so that they matter to us, so that we identify with them because they are like us. They carry on exactly the same struggle, encounter the same difficulties, doubts, and sorrows, the same hopes and joys. This is the spirituality I am speaking about, and this also means trusting that fraternity is the very basis of success in every struggle.

"Only if the poor see that we are really one — that we love one another — will they follow us."

## Chapter Twelve

# PRIEST, CITIZEN, AND DEFENDER OF HUMAN RIGHTS: ONLY ONE LIFE AND ONLY ONE STRUGGLE

### An Unusual Public Life

"Burying oneself and dying with the very poor also means coming back to life with them." As we have said, Father Joseph spent his life as part of an ongoing history that does not belong to him. It belongs to the poorest people and to God. "I sincerely believe that our Movement had to come into existence once these still undefended families had been revealed. Their state of abandonment in the Camp of Noisy-le-Grand, which soon became obvious in other emergency housing projects as well, could not help bringing forth new initiatives and a new analysis."

Still, wasn't it Father Joseph who introduced this new initiative and new outlook? He did not intend to portray history in this light. He did not say, "I have chosen, I have decided," but rather, "What else could I have done? Could I have formed an alliance with anyone else but with these families? They were already showing their perseverance while all along the Ministry of the Interior was refusing to grant its approval. We were living in a situation that was, so to speak, not exactly illegal — since we were not harming anyone — but rather beyond the reach of the law. I felt I was getting myself into a long struggle. Although we were already looking for more, the promotion of the families' dignity and basic security required that we at least begin to implement these three goals: to live in surroundings fit for human beings; to enable everyone to learn as much as possible; and to be recognized by other citizens. Founding an association was a risk we had to take, since doing nothing was out of the question."

This was how a public life "beyond the reach of the law" started in the Camp of Noisy-le-Grand. Over the years, it would lose none of its originality. Father Joseph would always lead anyone who had to deal with him off the beaten path. "How could we do otherwise, since the very poor introduce an experience and ways of thinking and acting that have never yet been taken into account?" Father Joseph often apologized, "I was a poor man myself; I didn't dream that one day I would be dealing with cabinet ministers. This was not the world I was used to." On the day we wrote the first proposal requesting support from the Ministry of Public Health, a completely astonished Father Joseph remarked with a smile, "I would never have thought that one day, as a priest, I would be suggesting to the state that it collaborate with me. I had been only too familiar with the Church of my childhood, ignored and held in contempt by the state. I just could not imagine where the poorest families were going to lead me."

As a matter of fact, they did lead him first of all to something he expected when he became a priest. In the ministries in these early years, he encountered much mistrust, discredit, and rejection not only of his direct approaches but also of all the ideas he was introducing about his fellow citizens trapped in persistent poverty. The fact that he was speaking on their behalf added no weight to his arguments; quite the opposite! This population group was not supposed to know what would be in its own best interest. The very idea that it might be entitled to state its opinions seemed incongruous. The experts were doing all the talking. This, by the way, was why Father Joseph was looking for top-notch university people: if there have to be experts, let's make sure that they're the best! Even so, inside the administration overrun by concern about specialization, he discovered a world where rules prevailed over human beings — even over painfully needy children. "Conditions in this camp do not meet standard requirements for day-care centers." The very fact that they lived in inhuman conditions deprived children of access to the most elementary means of recreation and vacation: no more clay, no more games, no more outings.

Father Joseph was often received in ways that were chilly, not always polite, and sometimes humiliating. "I'm learning," he said; and he let the public officials he had to meet do most of the talking. A friend who sometimes accompanied him commented, "He tries to learn something even from people who humiliate him." He did not react to the scandalmongering of which he was a victim: "Father Joseph wants to maintain shantytowns... The action carried out in the Camp of the Château de France does not seem very desirable... Aiding and abetting criminals..." When he helped inhabitants of La Campa to rebuild shelters nearby when they were ordered to leave this shantytown, a memorandum was circulated within the administration: "Father Wresinski's organization is creating a new shantytown." He paid no attention to it and continued to go, not so much from one office to another as from one person to another, trying to build friendships. He could not act in any other way if he wanted to obtain the slightest change. He had no bargaining chips; he could only use persuasion. Yet it was not only the need to find supporters that made him seek out civil servants. His intention was not to challenge public officials; he went to meet the man or the woman with whom he could create a meaningful relationship. Later a Volunteer would say, "I discovered his faith in mankind by the way in which he met people. Each time, he addressed the human being rather than his or her position, with the steadfast concern of turning each person into a supporter of the cause of the very poor."

During the 1960s, he had to face a lot of hostility nonetheless. In 1962, a friend worried about the future of the Camp wrote, "The organization's modest achievements upset the powers-that-be. Some fear that a destitute population, which they would rather get rid of, is going to put down roots. Others think that providing such families with the means for action runs the risk of inciting them to civil disorder."

Father Joseph is going to speak to one and all with the same straightforwardness. "I am confident that you are not going to destroy the igloo-huts in the Camp or the shacks in the shantytown without offering decent housing to these families. In the meantime, we would need preschools, workshops..." A director in the Ministry of Health is outraged: "Here is a man who opposes me in every possible way and who, in addition, is coming to ask me for funding!" Father Joseph pays him a visit. "How can you expect me to act differently? I'm sure that you'll understand." The director is intrigued. But perhaps he expected as much. He has arranged to meet with Father Joseph after office hours. The ministry is empty. He keeps him a long time, sharing his personal worries with Father Joseph: "Of course, if I were surrounded by collaborators who could put together files the way you do..." They become friends. The first significant public funding dates from this moment.

## The Family, an Uphill Fight

By now, we are in the year 1964. The (so-called) Debré Law concerning the demolition and absorption of shantytowns represents a very fragile balance between the interests of the owners of the land and the interests of its inhabitants, who sought refuge there illegally. During this year, Father Joseph's struggle against persistent poverty publicly acquires its characteristic identity as a struggle for the family. In his opinion, his own role in this development is still a minor one. "Someone really had to start declaring that extreme poverty was not only a matter of housing or of isolated individuals, that it embraced a population of families. These families are, in fact, an entire segment of the population, including adults, children, and elderly — a whole people made up of families. This was bound to happen; the history of the very poor was carrying us along."

From 1960 on, in the magazine *Igloos*, he spoke about these families and about their desperate efforts to keep their children. In 1964, he called for a genuine rallying around families "with neither home nor hearth." "These families are not in a position to belong to any group or to any Church, since they can neither begin nor carry on a dialogue with anyone." The Movement would therefore have to be built up all the more strongly around them. Some people criticized him for his obstinate struggle for the family at a time when everyone's agenda pointed to furthering women's liberation. It seemed to be impossible to reconcile the two. However, "... the family obviously represents human beings' last bulwark, their last refuge. The family is the last defense against adversity, humiliation, rejection, and self-destruction." How could anyone overlook the fact that any policy against poverty must be a policy for the family? From the deepest depths of persistent poverty, Father Joseph was patiently sending out his appeals. "If the organization had ten thousand members, it would certainly be easier for us to make ourselves heard by public opinion and public authorities."

How does membership actually reach ten thousand, forty thousand, and even some one hundred thousand throughout the world? For the time being, the Movement's founder seems to continue leaving the beaten path, if not really the limits of legality. "Misery is not something to be shouted out; it is something to be discovered." The magazine *Igloos* becomes an authentic documentation resource. It is the first, and until now the only, magazine to give an account of the everyday experiences of the very poor in France and in Europe with growing accuracy and in-depth analyses. "The following pages are going to tell you about this suffering. Please forgive us. We wanted this document to be serious, because the poor should be taken seriously."

Little by little, his straightforwardness, his conviction, and the incisiveness of his files command respect. Yet, above everything else perhaps, his personality and his trust win people's friendship. Father Joseph is greatly pleased by this, but he remains clear-headed. " We are winning people over, hearts and minds. We are obtaining some preferential measures and some funds. We are not getting enough legislation passed. We have not secured top priority for the poorest. On their behalf, our society is still investing leftovers — funds that have remained unspent at the end of a fiscal year, obsolete equipment — where we should be innovating and investing the best."

In 1987, even after undeniable progress, he would not talk any differently. "We live in a society that does not keep its promises to the very poor. Our society never stops making political promises. But it does not keep them. This situation has been going on for thirty years and more in France, and it is still going on." This is why blaming the families for the number of children they have, which he would hear being done over the years, appeared to him to be all the more unacceptable. By what right could a society that did not keep its promises step in to control the most intimate dimensions of people's lives? At the end of 1965, this is how he expressed the pain and the outrage that would never let go of him. These are still the years when shantytowns are being absorbed in ways that, despite many promises, leave the most deprived families with nothing to call their own.

"And it came to pass, in those days, that people decided to destroy shantytowns. They held a census of all the wretched of the earth who happened to be in shantytowns and rough-and-ready housing projects. They said: 'We do not want to hurt you, but you have to understand that our cities must be beautiful and clean, and that everything in them must be in perfect order.' So people set out to build their new cities. But the names of people counted during the census no longer showed up on their rehousing lists. They had to stay in temporary emergency shelters. People asked them, 'Why are you staying there? What are you doing there? Do you like it there? Don't you see that your children are dirty and cold? Don't you understand that you are not fit to be their parents? We are going to take care of your children and place them elsewhere.'

"Then the poorest families left these temporary emergency shelters. They went back on the road, returning to where their forebears had lived — those who belonged to the race of the wretched. From one furnished hotel room to another, from temporary shelter to emergency housing project, they ended their journey once again where they had started it. Here they set up their hearth and built their shelter by raising a few boards on posted land — a landfill

*Father Joseph and others watch as bulldozers destroy shacks in the shantytown of La Campa, 1966.*

or private property — that until then had been uninhabited or that no one was taking care of any longer."

As Father Joseph saw it, the child born in the makeshift shelter found the shepherds of Bethlehem in his neighborhood. Through this child's soul, God would dwell in this broken land, called into being by tears and shame. How could the poorest people celebrate Christmas on their forsaken, battered lands in any way other than by bringing a child into the world? "For the wretched, is there any way of celebrating Christmas other than by bringing a son into the world?" When Father Joseph was strongly moved, the language of his childhood welled up in him. In those days, the very poor were called "the wretched."

It remained true that this struggle against persistent poverty, which required defending the child and the family, was not attuned to the political trends of that period. From the 1970s on, Father Joseph would take this untimely and uphill political struggle upon himself as a full-scale program. He had neither the taste nor the temperament for political life, but he set himself to it with determination. He could not do otherwise. "Opposition to this political struggle is widespread and long-lasting at all levels: within administrations, political parties, and churches. It may sometimes be disguised, but it is still real and broad-based." Such was the warning he gave to the Volunteer Corps over the years. "We are committed to the weakest of populations, and we are not exactly rock-solid ourselves. We are powerless; the families have to realize this. All we have is our affection; the kind of affection that we cannot keep to ourselves, that we must share so that it can mean something to the world... We still have only our word, our commitment, our life to throw into the balance. The very poor have no power whatsoever, and they cannot give us any. We are bound to use persuasion."

*With a family in the Val d'Oise, France, 1987.*

## An Atypical Political Program That Is Nevertheless Spreading Around the World

And when Father Joseph does talk about himself (once in a very long while), he says cheerfully: "I was a rather violent young man, and here I am, a man of consensus. I had no choice. The very poor are overwhelmed by violence; they are dreaming of peace. They know better than anyone else that their only weapon is their suffering." In these few words, we recognize a lifelong program as well as a political project that might be unprecedented and that, in any case, was atypical from the outset. At a time when many are talking about antagonistic relationships and class struggle, Father Joseph seems to be gambling that human suffering alone can win over hearts and minds and give rise to fair laws. On behalf of the poorest, he refused any kind of dependence on handouts, any kind of high-handedness. He refused to let them be subjected to any social action, of either a "therapeutic" or an "educational" type. He would set out to create places designed for "sharing knowledge and skills", centers for cultural development, Art and Poetry Clubs and, finally, People's Universities in order to lay the foundations of social partnership and political representation. All of this was carried out with families who, until then, had been considered of no significance in the life of their country. Did he really believe that love and trust could change the world? "If you love people, if you do nothing else but love people, you will be helping us," he wrote from his shack in the Camp of Noisy-le-Grand.

From this place that could hardly be reached by a paved road (the highway stopped at the first shacks), his relations spread out in ways no one could grasp. The Movement that he was building was not one of those that launch huge campaigns. However, men and women wrote to him from all over, talked to him about their struggles against poverty and called on him to visit them. They represented all kinds of backgrounds and a wide variety of beliefs. As for Father Joseph himself, he trusted them and he encouraged them to invest time and energy in the widest range of initiatives. The only thing that mattered to him was a person's sincerity. "Does your work take into account what the poorest people experience and hope for? What do they stand to gain from your projects?"

This trust, which nevertheless accepted no compromise at the expense of the most disadvantaged, would result in the creation of a Movement that included all the continents.

During the "Assises" in 1983, Father Joseph explains his outlook. "In a world where rich people are often condemned publicly, we believed in them... Trust is not something one deserves; trust is something to be given. No one is automatically trustworthy; each of us can become trustworthy. Trust should be spread; we can share it. Trust is the way in which we confide responsibility to someone. All the rest is just words. We have no enemies to knock down, only friends to win over."

As a matter of fact, Father Joseph did seem to be winning them over patiently, one by one. The struggle, which had been so fiercely challenged, was gaining members, ground, and fame. Little by little, new friends and Volunteers opened new paths for him in public life. Although he would never feel completely comfortable in this area, he did realize that there were steps only he could take.

Indeed, as soon as Father Joseph was called to other continents and his activity grew there, it became obvious that he represented the poorest people around the world. Thanks to him, starting in 1970, the Movement obtained consultative status, first with ECOSOC, then with UNESCO, the ILO, the Council of Europe, UNICEF, the U.N. Human Rights' Commission, and other agencies. All of this was accomplished in spite of limited means and a complete absence of financial reserves. Thanks also to Father Joseph's personal influence, ATD Fourth World soon acquired a special place among some five hundred non-governmental organizations (NGOs) that enjoy the same status. Not all the founders of NGOs met regularly with the U.N. Secretary General or the Secretary General of the Council of Europe. Not all the international NGOs were received for annual consultations by the Commission of the European Community or the general director of the ILO or UNESCO. Not all of them could speak before the Human Rights' Commission in Geneva. Father Joseph was granted this special place, because more and more he appeared to be the genuine representative of population groups actually experiencing major hardships.

Through him, we discover that the men and women heading intergovernmental organizations feel more strongly than we might imagine their own remoteness from the world's peoples. "We, the peoples of the United Nations..." Mr. Javier Perez de Cuellar, who becomes U.N. Secretary General in 1982, tries to give these words that introduce the United Nations' Charter a more realistic content. In 1982, Father Joseph is going to hand over to him an "Appeal to the Defenders of Human Rights," bearing 232,500 signatures. Mutual recognition and friendship spring up between the two men right away. Mr. Perez de Cuellar observes, "You are my eyes and ears in areas of human misery." Father Joseph replies, "Without the personal commitment of people like you, the families in deepest poverty will remain nameless unknowns, subjected to the humiliation of old-fashioned charity." Their friendship is going to last beyond death. Equally long-lasting will be his friendship with Francis Blanchard, Director General of the ILO, who will say later, "Father Joseph came to me to request what I was ready to grant him beforehand. He guided us in a struggle that I was endeavoring to pursue myself. With him, the poorest among the world's young people came inside our walls. It is up to us to carry on now."

*Javier Perez de Cuellar, then Secretary of the United Nations, greets Father Joseph in 1984. "You are my eyes and ears in areas of extreme poverty in the world."*

## Can the Poorest Be Partners?

As a matter of fact, Father Joseph does not go anywhere without introducing "inside institutions' walls" men, women, youth, or children held in contempt because of their extreme poverty. He does not want to let any misunderstanding cloud the identity of the population group he represents. While Volunteers and friends are preparing official steps to be taken, he is carefully ensuring that the very poor will be present in these public approaches, either in person or by their contribution to reports. He is still the priest who "puts out into deep water," and he is becoming increasingly the representative and advocate of those trapped in extreme poverty. Yet he remains above all the man who wants to see the very poor standing tall, "taking the lead on the way to the Kingdom," as well as being partners recognized by their fellow citizens.

It is with this aim in mind that he organizes a festival in the *Mutualité* Hall in Paris on November 17, 1977. Five thousand delegates and friends of the Fourth World proclaim, "Our goal over the next ten years is that no one among us should remain illiterate; that not only should no child miss school but also no child should fail in school; that all those who know how to read and write should teach their neighbors; that everyone should feel responsible for their own professional training." Two years later in 1979, two thousand children from underprivileged areas all over the world come to salute the Year of the Child in Paris. Another festival, "Full Rights for All People," follows at *Forest National* in Brussels in 1982. Ten thousand delegates and friends commit themselves there to defending human rights primarily for the very poor. Father Joseph heads a delegation of Fourth World families in a visit to Mr. Ivor Richards, Commissioner of Social Affairs in the European Economic Community. The same year, he accompanies fifty young people from areas of severe poverty to see Pope John Paul II in Castel Gandolfo. In 1985, one thousand Fourth World youths meet with Francis Blanchard. With civil servants looking on in amazement, they put on a show in the gardens of the International Labor Organization to declare their right to knowledge and to a trade. Last but not least, a huge gathering of human rights defenders occurs on October 17, 1987. One hundred thousand people from all over the world participate in the inauguration of the Commemorative Stone on the Plaza of Human Rights in Paris. On it are engraved these words, which recount Father Joseph's lifelong struggle:

*Father Joseph leads a delegation of young people from four continents to see Pope John Paul II in 1982.*

***October 17, 1987***

***On this day, defenders of human rights from every continent gathered on this Plaza. They paid homage to the victims of hunger, ignorance and violence. They affirmed their conviction that human misery is not inevitable.***
***They proclaimed their solidarity with people throughout the world who fight to eradicate extreme poverty.***

❖

***"Wherever men and women are condemned to live in poverty, human rights are violated. It is our sacred duty to come together to ensure that these rights are respected."***

***Father Joseph Wresinski***

Representing every nationality, culture and creed, the one hundred thousand participants in the October 17 event form a crowd where all the world's peoples seem to mingle. They are from all walks of life, the poorest families rubbing shoulders with cabinet ministers. They also represent the entire spectrum of political affiliations. Before the gathering on the Trocadero Plaza and at Father Joseph's request, the Church prays with destitute families in Notre-Dame Cathedral in Paris. On that day, mankind is united, and the very poor are its focal point. On that October 17, perhaps Father Joseph is the only person who does not believe that he has won. He signed the guest book at the ceremony with these words: "The poorest are waiting for us at the turning point. What are we going to do?"

Perhaps he was alone, along with his own people, in realizing the fragility of everything that had been obtained on their behalf. Ever since his childhood, ever since his stay in the Camp of Noisy-le-Grand, he had lost none of the lucidity of the very poor. Tomorrow, everything can be lost once more. As long as the very poor have no right to freedom of speech, no mastery, no control of their own whatsoever, everything can still be taken away from them again at any moment. The spirit of a law can be betrayed, the law itself fade into oblivion. Even the vital events of their own history can be erased from our common memory. So what is their rightful place? What is their right to freedom of speech? Who is really carrying on a history *with* them, on an equal footing? Who really wants the very poor as traveling companions? Who wants to invite them to their own table rather than to make sure they are fed by a food bank? Who really wants to see them living independently instead of giving them only enough to survive on: an odd job with no dignity or an unambitious vocational training in exchange for endless outside control?

On the evening of the vast October 17 gathering, Father Joseph proposes to the Volunteer Corps a year of silence, reflection, and meditation. He asks Christian Volunteers to leave for a pilgrimage with Fourth World youths every year on that same day. The Movement, "built by vulnerable people around vulnerable people," must be strengthened. From 1979 on, he himself has devoted a special effort to writing. Four books are offered to the Church, the Movement and the world between 1983 and 1986: *The Poor Are the Church,*[17] *Blessed Are You the Poor!,*[18] *The Poor, Meeting with the Real God,*[19] and *Compass for Tomorrow.*[20] All Father Joseph's important texts about human rights are also written in the 1980s. He senses that, both for the families and the Movement, the time has come to think and to assimilate.

Indeed, as the Movement advances, the long road still to be traveled stretches out even more clearly. "Until the end of time, even in Europe, will the very poor ever live in security?" Father Joseph, who is always optimistic and determined, still shows that he remains very worried about Europe. Was the European Community charting the right course toward a Europe of human rights? The "European Programs to Fight Against Poverty," which he helped to create in 1975, were soon lacking in vision as well as in financial backing. As early as 1957, he himself laid the groundwork for a Europe that would no longer be based on economics but on human beings. "Both the poorest and those who stood beside them had no choice. They had to unite, to shape a common European identity, in order to en-

17 An English translation is currently being prepared.
18 *Blessed Are You the Poor!*, Father Joseph Wresinski, Fourth World Publications, Paris, France, 1992, 287 pp.
19 An English translation is currently being prepared.
20 An English translation is currently being prepared.

dure and to speak out together." But on whose behalf should one speak out? Father Joseph worried about how the very poor were represented, in the 1980s as much as in the 1950s. At his request, inter-party Fourth World groups had been set up both in the French Chamber of Deputies and in the Senate, as well as in the European Parliament. Yet an understanding of the indivisibility of human rights was nowhere to be found. Faced with this void, Father Joseph was once more going to fulfill his responsibilities as a citizen.

## The Wresinski Report

In 1979, the President of the Republic appointed him a member of the French Economic and Social Council in the category of "leading personalities." He belonged to the Social Affairs Section, where he intervened discreetly but tenaciously on behalf of the very poor in France. Councillor Jean René Masson would comment, "For each report considered by the Section, Father Joseph was there to recall, in terms of one aspect or another, the need for an approach that would take account of the most disadvantaged." His colleague, Mrs. Lingelser, also remembers the quality of his presence. "Each time we went astray, he would say something so human that it would refocus us." Armed with patience, Father Joseph allowed himself six years to reach his goal: that the Council should initiate an in-depth study of extreme poverty. In 1985 it finally happened, and Father Joseph was appointed as rapporteur (reporter). For the next two years, he was going to mobilize families, the Volunteer Corps, hundreds of friends, politicians, civil servants, and heads of non-governmental organizations. The Fourth World People's Universities, which by now have spread across the country, took on their full meaning. With all the other partners in society, the very poor were going to contribute to the Report, *Chronic Poverty and Lack of Basic Security*. The rapporteur did not try to write a report in his own name, but rather to form a national consensus around the most disadvantaged families.

How did he succeed, without having to compromise either on the description of the facts or on the solutions to be found? When it adopted it Policy Statement on February 11, 1987, the Economic and Social Council immortalized the definition of poverty in terms of human rights, by which Father Joseph gave to the report a universal dimension. The Council proclaimed and demonstrated that extreme poverty is a violation of all human rights. It asserted that it could be ended only by a comprehensive, coherent, and forward-looking policy against poverty and for human rights, based on long-range legislative measures.

In this way, the Wresinski Report has become something like a charter for any country that wants to fight against extreme poverty. At the end of his life, Father Joseph offered it as a legacy to the world's poorest and to those seeking to live in solidarity with them. This is a political report, about which Jean René Masson states again, "As you wend your way through a chapter, its human side hits you right in the face." It became the Economic and Social Council's most popular report: more than twenty-five thousand copies distributed in two years on every continent. Invited to consultations by cabinet ministers, by heads of state and international organizations, Father Joseph remained true to himself: he did not introduce himself as the report's author. The Council itself soon called it "the Wresinski Report," and this term would acquire a generic meaning within international spheres: "Make a Wresinski Report for Italy, for Europe..." Yet the very man who exhausted himself in drawing it up, without abandoning his other responsibilities, remained clearheaded. He knew that history would remember this charter for the fight against extreme poverty only if the Economic and Social Council continued to vouch for it. Personally, he was happy that his text represented a reliable translation into political terms of his way of reading the Gospels. He had never intended to do anything else. He never made any compromises concerning what he believed, and he never wanted to be a politician, any more than he wanted to be a manager or an expert, for that matter.

While awarding him the officer's insignias of the National Order of Merit in 1986, Gabriel Ventejol, President of the Economic and Social Council, said about Father Joseph: "In his opinion, the very poor were not his own — nor even only his Church's — business. They were mankind's business. They could unite all people... Father Joseph does seem to be one of those people who prompt their contemporaries to carry on their part in history with bold forward strides. He was definitely not a prophet in his own country right away. He needed courage, perseverance, and lucidity to convince his fellow citizens, poor and non-poor alike, that it was time to innovate, to dare to try new methods of action and of representation, and even a new democracy. It is not only in the area of humanity... but also in the area of political life, that Father Joseph forced us to push back our limits. He did not consider himself to be a forerunner; he always wanted to be a witness to what people are capable of accomplishing at a given moment in history, a servant of the best they have to contribute to their own era."

## "Have I Been Faithful?"

When this kind of homage was paid to him (in 1976, he had already been made a knight of the Legion of Honor), Father Joseph invariably replied, "What an opportunity for the families! They are the ones whom society is honoring." In public life, he kept uppermost in his mind the strong desire to remain faithful to his priestly calling. "'You shall worship Him only!' I have had to keep repeating that to myself more and more often... In becoming a member of the French Economic and Social Council, in meeting heads of state regularly, in addressing important United Nations' meetings, in obtaining public aid from the European Economic Community or the Council of Europe, I had my place — be it ever so modest — in public life. Was I then still true to the choice of Jesus? Fourth World families are my people. I cannot imagine life without them. But am I still with them as the Gospel demands? Am I still the voice of my people who suffer and hope? Is the prestige I achieved — if any — *their* prestige, *their* dignity recognized at last?"

Until the end of his days, Father Joseph would put back into the families' hands the successful outcome of his lifetime of efforts as a man, a priest, and a citizen. Had it all been enough: his sorrow in witnessing their sorrow, his anguish in knowing them to be in anguish, his sleepless nights spent in a family where too much suffering had caused violence to break out, as well as his efforts to reach out to a world that was not his own? Had it all been enough? Had he loved his own enough?

*Public lecture at the Sorbonne, "Defeating Persistent Poverty." Paris, 1983.*

# Chapter Thirteen

# "I AM CONFIDENT"

## "The Church Trusted Us"

We have watched Father Joseph becoming a well-known public figure. Still, ever since his total immersion in the Camp of Noisy-le-Grand, what has his place in the Church become? When he left his parishes in the Department of the Aisne, he left behind a recognized status without getting another one in exchange. Father Douillard, Bishop of Soissons, had learned that people were asking for the presence of a priest in a camp for homeless families. What were the reasons for this request; what goal was this presence supposed to fulfill? Abbé Pierre had created this place, but he had not intended to live there or to undertake any pastoral action with its inhabitants. Two other priests had attempted to approach these families. Both of them had given up. No Church mission or organized religious life had been established in this camp. Who even knew exactly what to ask of a priest on behalf of these very poor but also very demoralized families?

"My bishop told me, 'You can stay as long as you want to. You remain assigned to the diocese, and you can come back any time.' He did not know any more about it than I did; he gave me the freedom to choose. I built everything on his trust." Father Joseph would always be proud of this trust, not for his own but for the Church's sake. He would often talk about this Church, which was strong only in her weakness and her trust. He devoted a stubborn confidence to her in return. Often questioned about how the Church supported him, Father Joseph always answered with the same firmness, "The Church left me free; she could not have done more. I had gone off the beaten path. The Church trusted me."

Still, could the Church not have helped him better when he was alone, powerless, and misunderstood, when he was going hungry? "If the Church has not supported us through her structures, she has not tried to lead us back into the fold either. She had too much respect for us." Besides, Cardinal Marty will remind him of this, and Father Joseph keeps his words in his heart. "You wanted to create a Movement where people of all beliefs would gather together around the very poor. The best way to help you was to accept this from the start and to allow you to follow your own path." And Monsignor Marty will add: "Perhaps this Movement, which is not of the Church, is still an authentic expression of the Church of tomorrow?" Father Joseph, who does not believe himself to be a precursor, is happy about this. He is convinced that the very poor always bring the Church back to her very essence. And he loves this Church that, in the end, always allows herself to be guided by them. He stands up for her: "It is right to state that the Church has never doubted our sincerity. The Church has never stopped trusting us."

In January 1965, he writes, "Let us disregard the history of her charities, her works of mercy, and her organizations for assistance. Let us just listen to the heartbeat of each priest in his parish and of each sister in her convent. For whom are their hearts beating if not for the very poor? All those who have come to see me in Noisy-le-Grand have, in one way or another, expressed their desire to be present in the midst of human misery or their anxiety about not being present there."

Does Father Joseph convey an angelical outlook? Has the Church really done what she could; has she never hindered him? Gilles Anouil floods him with questions during his interviews for *The Poor Are the Church.* Still Father Joseph does not accept hasty judgements. "The Church preached caution and patience to the priests and laity scattered around poor areas... They are more numerous than people realize; extreme poverty is always a focal point for gathering human beings... Perhaps they do not always do what should be done, but anyone who has met with chronic poverty is marked for life. Rare are those who do not become advocates of justice or advocates of peace. You may be assured that the Church did not merely let them act in their own names. She gave them the freedom to fully share in the lives of the most disadvantaged. Of course, we would like the Church to be more active and closer to those who try to reach families who are engulfed by extreme poverty. These people sometimes despair at the apparent pointlessness of their efforts."

## Announcing God's Forgiveness to People Whom the World Finds Guilty

When he speaks like this, Father Joseph is not referring to his own situation. He has chosen a community of common destiny with the very poor and "sharing in their sufferings this way was probably a good thing for the families." He has been able to remain not only a priest but also a pastor over the years. This is the essential point. "In the Camp of Noisy-le-Grand, the very poor were not just part of my parish. Several hundred families, living in a state of complete abandonment, became my parish. Actually, they took control of my life and became my unfailing teachers.

"They were families whom human misery caused to wander along the highways of France, and who had 'nowhere to lay their heads.' Families banished from French society just as the Holy Family had been from Hebrew society in Herod's time. Mothers who had only a crate or a piece of cardboard found in the marketplace on which to lay down their new-born babies. Workers who were unemployed or surviving on odd jobs, and children who were taken away from their family because it was too severely impoverished. Men and women whom an entire neighborhood had carefully kept at a distance, next to whom people avoided sitting on the bus.

*Father Joseph in Noisy-le-Grand with a group of children in the early 1960s. "Among the thousands of children I have known, all of them held on to that innocence which refused to disappear, the wholesome outlook which could neither judge nor condemn."*

"As a priest in the emergency housing camp of Noisy-le-Grand, I was living right inside the Gospel, with the lepers, the demoniacs, the Samaritan woman, the man born blind, the sick man whom no one helped to reach the Pool of Bethesda at the right moment. I was living with these poorest members of an impoverished people, whom Jesus never ceased to draw forth out of exclusion, putting them in the middle of the crowds, in the middle of the struggle, if I may say so, as first witnesses and first partners of a Kingdom that had already been fulfilled in our Lord's lifetime.

"Here is where I understood that it was definitely not enough to dive deeply into poverty, and even less to do it alone. Jesus had enabled the very poor to stand up tall: You have been saved, go and sin no more. In other words, since you have been saved, go and work to bring about God's Kingdom from now on. This was my first task, and it still is: telling the poorest families, 'You have been saved; now become people who bear witness to the Kingdom. Go encourage and defend those who are even poorer and more excluded than you are.'

"Conveying God's forgiveness and salvation was, and still is, essential wherever extreme poverty crushes people and families ... instilling in them a lasting feeling of guilt and shame. This is even truer since society at large does not fail to remind them constantly of their limitations and weaknesses. How could my first concern as a priest not be to announce God's forgiveness to these families who were considered guilty just as the very poor were considered 'unclean' in Jesus' time?"

This is how Father Joseph addresses the Convention of Catholics (Katholikentag) in his talk, "Thy Kingdom Come," at Aix-la-Chapelle, Germany, 1986. Already in 1985, *Prayer* magazine had selected a similar statement: "Their entire lives are so many calls to mercy: 'I did not mean to hit my wife,' or, 'I did not mean to fight with my husband.' Day after day this question keeps coming back: 'Is it my fault ... tell me, it's not really my fault, is it? '" Then the magazine adds, "No one has ever talked like Father Joseph about this need for rehabilitation and forgiveness that dwells in those who have reached the bottom of human misery: 'Incredible hardships, which people experience as their own fault ...' In his eyes, the Fourth World is a part of the Eucharist that constantly revives Christ's Passion, as well as his Resurrection."

## Do Not Challenge the Church, but Rather Embody Her Challenge to the World

It should come as no surprise that Father Joseph walks through the Gospels in complete harmony with his Church. In the light of his personality and his life, questions about the Church's faithfulness are somehow pointless. In 1987, he tells the magazine *Sign of the Times*, "Christians should not challenge their Churches. Standing at the very center of their Churches, they should embody and spell out the Churches' challenges. When I protest because today there are one hundred thousand sixteen-year-olds who leave school without knowing how to read and write, it is not just one person who is protesting — it is an entire Church, which is my native land as well as the source from which I draw my life's breath and passion."

One of his favorite prayers while celebrating holy mass is, "Do not consider our sins, but rather the faith of your Church." Here is how we hear him pray on June 1, 1986, during a meeting of supporters of the Movement in Pierrelaye, France:

> "In Your tenderness, Lord, keep in Your heart
> the little ones, the humble ones, the people of no account...
> those who wear themselves out serving others,
> who are criticized and forgotten.
> Keep in Your heart the least-of-all,
> the humble, the poor,
> the priests' housekeepers,
> women in charge of catechism,
> reciters of the rosary,
> who are the bedrock and life blood of Your Church.
> In Your tenderness, Lord, forget no one,
> none of those who suffer, who are afraid,
> none of those who are in love
> and who need You so much to live out their love.
>
> Welcome home all human beings, Lord.
> They are all Your children.
> Do not consider their sins,
> But rather the faith of Your Church,
> the prayers of Your Church,
> the true love of Your Church.

Welcome them home beside the Virgin Mary,
the exquisite, the wonderful,
the extraordinary Virgin Mary,
the Mother of Your Son,
beside Joseph whom we do not talk about much..."

We should not expect a priest who prayed this way to lend his support to any challenges directed toward the Church.

## The Permanent Forum on Extreme Poverty: Gathering Together Those Who Are Fighting Alone Outside Our Walls

Still, not all his colleagues in the Church understood him. This saddened him but did not make him lose his bearings. What disturbed him was the loneliness of other priests and laity facing the same difficulties as he did. Many of them came to see him. One day in the 1960s, he asked Father Rodhain, the Founder of Caritas, for an appointment. Could he not help them by giving them the material assistance which they lacked so cruelly? They could obtain such aid only through endless appeals to public charity. Wasn't this additional anxiety unnecessary?

"Nothing came of it, and there were many who continued to vegetate and exhaust themselves in trying to draw the poor out of their condition. Seeing them forced, like me, to beg constantly for funds to support their efforts made me suffer. In fact, this led us to create 'Science and Service Clubs'[21] to support them."

Indeed, Father Joseph's worries led him to take action. The first Volunteers remember the visit that Mrs. Magnan of La Rochelle paid to the Camp of Noisy-le-Grand. All by herself, she was supporting families who had sought refuge in unused German bunkers along the coast. She would return home with several thousand francs that had been set aside for renovating the playground used by the children of the Camp. Just like Mother Theresa, who had

[21] Science and Service Clubs were formed of groups of concerned citizens from all walks of life, affiliated with the Fourth World Movement. Their main goal was to work with the Fourth World Movement to prepare society to welcome back the most disadvantaged families as full-fledged partners in the struggle to end extreme poverty.

come to talk with Father Joseph at about the same time, would leave the Camp with the most beautiful crucifix from the chapel.

During the 1960s, in fact, the Movement that had started in Noisy-le-Grand was going to provide a meeting place for hundreds of small organizations and thousands of people committed to standing beside abandoned population groups throughout the world. There they would encourage one another and exchange experiences. Nearly one fourth of them are Christian: sisters entrenched in a disadvantaged neighborhood, more neglected than others, somewhere in Latin America; a priest working inside a prison on the outskirts of a city South of the Sahara... They had learned about Father Joseph through friends or religious magazines. Having once had nothing but his priest's cloak to keep himself warm, he could not endure their loneliness and their deprivation. Little by little, he created a huge network of personal correspondence. He also went out looking for people who were struggling like this, all by themselves, in areas of extreme poverty, unnoticed by the world. "Science and Service Clubs" evolved into the Permanent Forum on Extreme Poverty, which also became the launching pad for sending Volunteers toward four continents. In 1988, it included some five thousand members, individuals or small organizations.

*Philippines, 1987.*

This was how Father Joseph, moving forward outside the walls of the Church, gathered together those who, like himself, were in the middle of nowhere, exposed to all the ups and downs of human misery as were the very poor themselves. Thanks to him, they are no longer unknown; they meet regularly at UNESCO. Above all, they share in a training program, regardless of their nationalities and beliefs. Moreover, Father Joseph is very careful to give them back to the Church, as it were, since he never goes anywhere without notifying the bishop of the diocese he is visiting or without asking for his advice and his support. Even outside her walls, he is still building the Church, still leading his own people back toward her. And it is in her name, and in the name of all those believers scattered around the four corners of the earth, that he refuses to let her image as the Church of the poor be distorted by unfair criticism. Father Jean Pardon, his colleague from the diocese of Soissons, would remember this after Father Joseph was called back to God: "Like so many others when faced with blatant injustices, you could have accused the Church of always siding with the strongest, of hobnobbing with everyone in power, of being the Church of the rich. Yet, Joseph, you declared with a loud voice and with such love: The Church is the poor! You proved it abundantly, not only with your writings but also with your life and the lives of those whom you carried along in your wake."

In fact, Father Joseph becomes not only a witness but also an advocate of thousands of men and women who are embodying the Church in the most forgotten areas of the world. He does not defend a particular idea about the Church; he vouches for the Church of Jesus Christ, the wretched. He does not allow believers to malign the Church. That would amount to offending Jesus Christ himself and also to betraying the hopes of the most disadvantaged. If Fourth World families are not in the very heart of Christian communities, who is responsible for this? If believers themselves accuse the Church of this, what hope is left for these families?

## Giving the Very Poor Back to the Church

Father Joseph assumes responsibility himself: "I have always dreamed of giving the very poor back to the Church." Not everyone understood what he meant by that. Was it not rather the Church that had to be given back to the very poor? In his opinion, the Church belonged to them. If the very poor were not at the center of her concerns, her parishes, and her cathedrals, then were these latter really the Church? "The working-class world is not a homogeneous entity. It has its hidden side — that part of its mutilated body which is the Fourth World. Jesus Christ is lying low there, waiting for his priests. It is said that we should be among the working class, because it is the world of hope. We are all in agreement about this. Yet beyond it, there is a world of despair, the world of the down-and-out who require complete self-denial from us. We can approach them only by laying ourselves bare; we can defend them only by committing ourselves totally; we can share in their lives only by giving them our own. Do the most downtrodden among workers not represent the world of love, where Christ is fully at ease because this world is above all his own? From this world, the Church can expect everything, because, like her, the very poorest are not 'of the world' and they need to be delivered from evil."

With this world, the Church shares in a common destiny. "Just as the world does not want a poor Church at the service of humanity, so also it does not want the very poor to be seen and recognized as such. It tries to apply to them adjectives likely to make people consider them as responsible for their situation. Jesus was treated in exactly the same way. He had to be guilty and not a victim."

By "giving the poor back to the Church," Father Joseph means giving the Church back to herself, making her become fully the Church because the poorest will be the first served at the banquet table. He hopes that more and more priests, sisters, and laity will go "into the streets and alleys of the town ... to the open roads and the hedgerows." (Luke, Ch. 14, v. 21-23) to share in their life. Jesus was the first to do this. Referring to Saint Paul's words about Jesus Christ, Father Joseph reminds us, "It is He who has borne our infirmities and has carried our illnesses." "Must we invent limits to taking responsibility for infirmity and disease? Could Jesus take up the infirmity of the possessed without taking up their state of rejection, the horror and fright they aroused? Could he take on the suffering of the lepers and of the bleeding woman without sharing the stigma attached to their diseases? Jesus answers these questions first, not by lecturing but through His way of life."

*J. and B. Jahrling's marriage, 1978.*

Coming across statements like these, we understand a little better perhaps how Father Joseph endured — not without suffering but without ever complaining — the insults and attacks he was subjected to during the early years in the Camp. That also was a part of life in the midst of the Gospel represented to him by daily existence among families so unfairly condemned. Françoise and Marc Séjourné, who interviewed him in 1985 for *Prayer* magazine, are amazed by this:

> I asked him to share some of his prayer with me. His round face, his kind gaze turned toward another reality, more present than the room cluttered with papers and folders where we were meeting. Then, quietly, as if he were alone, he began to speak:
>
> 'When the Lord sets us down in the middle of human misery, he is not necessarily expecting words from us... He is compelling us to live in a constant state of humility. We have nothing to expect from human beings; we expect everything from God.
>
> 'Completely engulfed by this world, you are considered like someone who is eccentric and questionable. This is a condition that Christ did more than just accept: he desired it.
>
> 'One cannot begin to imagine what the poorest are telling us. We must look at things through the eyes of the Lord, through eyes filled with compassion, loving-kindness, indulgence, eyes that are never accusatory. *I am gentle and humble in heart:* that is the prayer of the Lord who can understand, share with and forgive both rich and poor alike...
>
> 'In order to be convincing, among the poor just as much as among the rich, we must pray humbly. Such is the prayer the Lord asks of us in the very heart of human misery. What matters is not so much our words as our attitude. *Who am I, Lord, beside you who are present within this world of human misery...?* Jesus Christ was not playacting. He was not pretending to be extremely poor, hungry, and dirty or to be smelling the odors of people surrounding him. This was not just a game, but truly a way of sharing in all that he held in the highest esteem, namely the love of God.
>
> 'Christ was not looking for anything for himself. He was not trying to make a name for himself. It was the poor who gave a name above all other names to him who humbled himself to the point of hearing other people say: *This man is a fool.'*

## Refusing Both Exclusion and Annexation

Father Joseph built a chapel in the Camp of Noisy-le-Grand as a place to welcome the prayers of the rich as well as those of the poor. "What other place could succeed better than this one in bringing together believers in the contemplation of Jesus, humiliated and rejected?" Then again, "How could anyone come from Paris to pray in this chapel unless it was as a way to tell the families that they were expected elsewhere?" Over the years, Father Joseph was host to a growing number of believers, both laity and religious, among whom more than two hundred would become full-time Volunteers. Still, he patiently discouraged any religious activity that would be on the fringes of the Church. He opposed the creation of communities of poor people. "When he founded Catholic Action for Workers (*Action catholique ouvrière*), Father Cardijn did not intend to create barriers behind which each social group would look for its own salvation. Such barriers are unknown in the Church. Humanity will find salvation with the very poor. They are its great opportunity; humanity should be given a chance to take advantage of it."

However, merely 'annexing' the poor would not provide the Church with its great opportunity either. Father Joseph will also be very cautious with respect to prayer groups or pilgrimages run by friends of the Movement who do not understand that they need serious training for these kinds of activities. Can they really enable these families to express themselves in a new language without getting trapped into using a language of the Church which is not their own? "The poor have their own God; we should not force them to pretend to believe in a God who is not their own. The God whom the very poor know intimately is not the same one that our cultural traditions have handed down to us. They do not read the Bible and the Gospels as we do."

Even during the years spent in the Camp of Noisy-le-Grand, he created a first study group on poverty and religion ("The Church and Underprivileged Families"). If in Tergnier he had started a Young Christian Workers group in a laundry room, in Noisy-le-Grand he would launch research about very poor people's spiritual life in a shed where old mattresses were used as seats by social scientists.

These basic goals — of not excluding the very poor, of not annexing people to serve one's own purposes, of finding a truly new place for them within our communities — form a challenging program. Father Joseph gathers together friends from all walks of life. As far back as the 1960s, he wove a fabric of connections across France and around the world thanks to endless personal correspondence. "Writing letters did not represent a chore. Each new correspondent was a potential friend; each person was a person to win over, an indispensable ally." He also communicates with each of them through the *Igloos* magazine, which for a long time will be printed on a second-hand, broken-down duplicating machine set up inside a shed in the Camp. For each issue, he writes an article on a religious topic, but the magazine is not limited to an audience of believers. It conveys a message, the same one for everyone, whatever their beliefs may be: "Let my people go ..." "Come to serve, to hear and then to seek out the oppressed, the lame, the blind, those whom the world has labeled as the down-and-out, martyred children, the Holy Innocents and their mothers who are crying because their children are wrenched away from them. Without all of them, what are your battles worth? Without them at the head of the table, where is the banquet? Besides, how will you know which seat to offer them, if you have not contemplated them?"

*Senegal, 1987. Father Joseph writes in the guest book of Gorée Island, where people were held before being taken away as slaves.*

Be that as it may, the "parish" of the Camp of Noisy-le-Grand is outward bound. A people is freeing itself from slavery. With Father Joseph, an entire people is putting out into deep water, reaching out to the world at large. A people who will stir up quite a breeze as it moves by. As a friend in the Vatican put it in 1982, "When he pays us a visit, we can feel the trade winds."

## A Movement of Every Creed, Because God Is Unity

The point is not only to give the very poor back to the Church, but also to give them back to the world. So continuous growth is going to lift up this Movement of people from all social backgrounds and religious beliefs, which many will find so hard to understand for a long time. Its founder charts the course; he offers neither theories nor recipes. He embodies unity and creates it all around him.

It is true that, in Father Joseph's eyes, gathering all human beings together remains first and foremost the act of a priest and of the Church. "I had experienced the good fortune that Catholics and Christians in general have; their upbringing prepares them to love others. I felt that we had to offer to everyone this opportunity that we, believers, had. In my opinion, enabling one and all — whatever their faith, beliefs, or education — to reach the very bottom of the social ladder was a question of justice. It is hard to imagine how awkward this is for those who have not enjoyed the privilege of growing up in the environment where we, who belong to a Church, have been educated."

Then does this whole endeavor, carried out by a Catholic priest, not lead to a movement within the Church? Father Joseph prefers to think of it as a movement of every religion, belonging to all people of goodwill. "Just because you are off the beaten path does not mean that you come from nowhere. We all come from our own backgrounds; only the very poor draw us together. We are drawn together by our determination that they become the driving force inside all our religions and beliefs. We come from all Churches, and we will be useful to them to the extent that we constantly provide them with an understanding of the religious practice, the prayers and the God of the very poor. In fact, the Churches are still in charge of evangelization. We are only links in the chain. But we are also a guarantee against mere annexation as much as against marginalization. The Volunteer Corps, which goes off the beaten path, guarantees the return of the poorest through the front door."

"Still, are you not dragging us into an adventure that is going nowhere?" a friend from the Netherlands asks him. "In our country, life is split into factions, and everyone has to choose a label." Father Joseph does not think so: "We are not setting out on an adventure; we are pledging confidence. I am confident. You are confident yourself, since you are here. God pays no attention to our labels. Is he not the God who draws people together, the same one who promises the unity of all scattered peoples? Read St. John again! God has already brought about this gathering; it exists. It is a mystery hidden from the wise, but the poor grasp it right away. All we need to do is to serve and to contemplate them. Unity has become a reality around these people who are His Son."

It is safe to assume that Father Joseph could trust the Church and mankind because he was sure about God. He was able to put the outcome of his life on earth into their hands, because God himself was the first to do this. When he said, "History was carrying us along," he was thinking about the history of God with his people. Between God and him, it was not a matter of trust but rather of a certainty that passes our understanding. God was his certainty, even when he sometimes grew despondent waiting for God to intervene to put an end to so much misery. His trust in human beings mirrored the wager that God himself placed on his children.

Father Joseph speaks so abundantly in his books of this God who gave himself over to human beings out of love for them. The trust born of that love demands that others be free to grow. Love, freedom, and trust are inseparable. Many have been astonished by Father Joseph's way of putting them into practice. He enables every person to grow; he wants each one to develop beyond what he himself has achieved. He enables families who have been the most completely crushed by human misery to pick up the pieces and to stand up again. "The Holy Spirit dwells in them too!" How did he dare to stake so much on the innate greatness of each person? This will remain his secret, the secret of an alliance that we are not able to understand, about which he never speaks, but which does speak through all his prayers. These prayers, both so spontaneous and so filled with the Holy Scripture, were the source of his strength, and he offered them to us to help us to pray with the very poor too.

"Our Father...
Yes, we are talking to You
like Jesus could teach us to,
because He was possessed with love for His Father,

because He lived out the relationship
with His Father...

Our Father,
because we have been saved
and are therefore standing tall,
new, risen human beings who have the means
to fulfill Your Kingdom...

Jesus taught us not merely
to put ourselves into Your hands at all cost,
not merely to be obedient to You,
but to be in harmony with Your heart.
You, our Father, the lasting reference for the world,
and we, Your children,
praying night and day,
listening, asking for advice,
but also questioning,
demanding,
giving You suggestions... .

Give us this day our daily bread,
give it to us every day.
You made it our duty to ask for it,
not as if we were pleading,
but to remind You that You are duty-bound
to give us bread,
because You are worried sick
that each person gets enough to eat.
You have known so many families, children,
forsaken men and women dying of starvation by the roadside.

You have seen so many mothers and fathers fighting,
spitting in each others' faces,
accusing each other and splitting up,
because there was no bread in the house.
Yes, Lord, You have seen all of that
and You could not accept it.
You are forced to give abundantly,
to give bread, and therefore work,
education in schools

a profession within everyone's reach...
Bread does not mean
being a jack of all trades and master of none... .

Our Father, You cannot cut Yourself off
from all these peoples around the world,
deprived of resources for development,
starving,
completely reduced to depending on others.
They are Your people
whom You have chosen for all eternity.
Through Jesus Christ, You became
the Father of all peoples,
Your Covenant has spread
to all the world's peoples.
You cannot abandon them.

Lord, a father is someone who
loves his children even more,
the more they are unhappy;
who stands more closely by his children,
the more they are in need...

The evil which You must deliver us from
is the evil of Your absence.
Jesus himself cannot accept it;
He cannot live beyond close intimacy with His Father.
Wherever the Father is absent, the Son cannot exist.
Deliver us from the evil of Your absence.
Our Father, You cannot abandon us..."

## A Passion for Humanity

Father Joseph is certain about God, the father of Jesus Christ, and about His plan for all human beings. Is this not what Jean-Claude Caillaux, a full-time Volunteer, theologian and exegete by training, explains in the April 1988 issue of *Convergence* magazine?

He was a free man; a free man, because he was a man of God. This freedom, this deep-seated humanity that he

> drew from springs of living water flowed not only into him but also into all who approached him, whether they were Christians or not... He knew how to share in another person's love; he knew how to share in another person's suffering. His look, his way of speaking that was sometimes a little rough as if he wanted to hide some feeling that was already perceptible anyway, the movements of his arm and his hand that hugged you as if he wanted to make you feel that your hope and suffering were his own... If I could, I would say he was a "man of people," like we say a "man of God."
>
> Indeed, he did believe in human beings. He was ready to trust anyone who crossed his path, because he was convinced that in all people, whoever they might be and whatever their status and responsibilities in society, their ideology, their professional commitments, their involvement with trade unions, political parties or other organizations, there was a determination that persistent poverty must be ended.
>
> This passion for human beings led him to disregard all boundaries that could have separated them. In his opinion, nothing should stand in the way of the urgency of people coming together, especially of their coming together around the very poor. Better still, he was convinced that the most humiliated among families were a rallying point and a gathering place for all, that they embodied the very leaven of peace, which everyone was constantly looking for.

Father Joseph has communicated to the Volunteers this trust and this desire for communion with every human being. These qualities stem from his faith, but also from the inner recesses of chronic poverty. "To what else could families aspire — deprived as they are of relationships through which to share with other human beings and with God — than to a world of communion? 'Let everyone join hands.' Is this not the hope that comes to light in their Notebooks of Petitions and their People's Universities?" He is happy to see the Volunteer Corps grow stronger in this aspiration, "with complete candor and innocence," as he likes to say.

Among these women and men of every belief, he deeply loved the atheists. Their suffering and their dismay over human misery are the most intense. Their generosity and their humility are the most remarkable also.

"Just imagine," he told a religious conference in Antwerp, Belgium, "imagine that out of love for the poorest, they accept closeness with a Church they do not like. And they go even further! Out of love for families despised by everyone, they are able to hope for a Church that will honor them. They are able to go and urge the parish priest to take care of catechism for children in an emergency housing development."

## To What Extent Should God Be Shared?

This Volunteer Corps, capable of generosity and humility, is going to lead Father Joseph little by little to clarify his most cherished dream for the Church. Because he does have a dream, which shows the full extent of his ambition for the most humiliated among people. Over the years, he constantly raises the question, "But what exactly are your ambitions for these families?" He puts this question to Volunteers as well as to governments, to the Economic and Social Council, to churches, and to non-governmental organizations. "Future generations will judge us by the ambitions that we will have shared with the very poor. Does our sense of solidarity go as far as true partnership? Does our sense of brotherhood go as far as sharing God? And to what extent are we going to share God?" In Father Joseph's opinion, just how far must this sharing go? Father Jean Lecuit, a Jesuit, discovers the answer over the years:

"I met Father Joseph for the first time in January 1973. From that first conversation, I remember only one comment. 'From the age-old trunk of religious life in the Church, new buds should sprout...' When this concern was entrusted to the priest and brother that I am, it gave me a glimpse into Father Joseph's priestly heart; it showed me the scope of his dreams... This dream went deep. How many times in fifteen years have I not heard him talk about contemplative life in the midst of the very poor? In order to have a Carmelite convent built, he would immediately have bought land next to a housing development for family advancement."

Father Joseph never gave up on this dream, even if, little by little, it became tinged with the fear that we have mentioned, fear of the often strong temptation to take possession of the very poor to serve our own purposes. Yet in his mind, the Church that returns to an area of extreme poverty is not taking advantage of its inhabitants in any way. She is going back home, and it is the very poor who are taking advantage of her. In the last chapter of his book, *The Poor Are the Church,* Father Joseph confides to Gilles Anouil, "All through our conversations, I have expressed the wish that haunts me: that the Church identify with this hateful and repulsive human misery of our time, that she identify once again with her true nature, enabling herself to be loved by the poorest and passing on to the world this deeply felt and shared love. I want her message to the world to be filled with this love that the poor will feel for her because in the Church they will have recognized Christ's face, bewildered, swollen, and stained by spit. This is the very Christ who has risen...

"The Church is completely helpless in a world where she cannot dictate her point of view and where people often ridicule her message. Left to themselves, the very poor are equally dependent. Together, they can rediscover from age to age that only love matters...

"You are asking me whether a special vocation and mission are necessary? I would reply first of all that those who are ordained are, in any case, called to love God in the poorest members of humanity. Not through this new, organized form of charity that has been bestowed upon the Church as a substitute for almsgiving... I am thinking of priests, monks and nuns sent by a Church whose reason for existing is forgiveness.

"Among them, the contemplatives are in a unique position. From the very beginning in Noisy-le-Grand, I have waited for the arrival of men and women whose sole concern would be to pray, worship, contemplate, and provide silence and peace. A peace that one could touch. You cannot imagine how much the Fourth World families need it. Introducing this element of stability and peace into their disturbed world is essential... I have so often wondered what was the use of the Church's praying, worshipping, and singing the glory of God while carrying the prayers of the poor, if the poor do not know about this and cannot join in with the Church... This presence is entirely possible; and thinking it is not does great harm to the poor. How could the Church forget that the hands of a mother sifting through garbage are the most beautiful hands when joined together in prayer?"

Here, Father Joseph is revealing his innermost hope, the hope in whose name, over the years, he has welcomed priests and nuns alongside Volunteers. "We must give them time," he used to say, "and encourage them above all to go back to their origins, to their founders' spirituality." Thanks to him, several religious orders have rediscovered in this way their founder and the inspiration and prayers on which they were established. Personally, he was confident that the Church would go beyond assistance and philanthropy, provided that she agree to take the path of silence and contemplation. "The Eucharist is not God's surplus; it is God himself. And to partake in the Eucharist with the very poor is not to provide them surplus goods through a food bank; it is not a way to avoid their presence by handing out our surplus. My priesthood is my real native country, and my native country is in the center of suffering mankind."

Still in this year of 1983, he also reveals a concern that he had not felt yet in the Camp of Noisy-le-Grand. "The Church has received a mission, but it is a mission beyond human capacities." The Church has to bear witness to the fact that the most disfigured human beings, the most shattered families, are filled with the Holy Spirit, called to prayer and to contemplation, destined to reach those summits where they can breathe freely. But the Church has a road to travel, the road leading back to Jesus Christ, who is wretched not in words but in point of fact, a "truly wretched person." The Church has to learn about this road and train herself to follow it.

As Jean-Claude Caillaux puts it once again, Father Joseph's way of thinking was growing "more explicit." Both his writings and his library bear witness to this. The latter had expanded since the time when "Reverend Joseph" used to move his books from one parish to another in a single crate. His library bears witness to his impassioned search for the history of the Church, of the poor, and of the working classes... Father Joseph saw the Church and the world moving toward a truly new awareness of extreme poverty and of solidarity with its victims. He contributed enthusiastically to this deepening of humanity's outlook and involvement. Yet the cautiousness of the very poor person he still remained was always rising to the top again. "They will have a lot of trouble wanting what God wants. What means will the Church use to train herself?"

## Contemplation and Prayer in the Heart of Extreme Poverty

"If the poorest start to teach us new ways of thinking, our conception of mankind will no longer be the same. If the Church considers that the lowly and the hungry 'exalted' in Mary's Magnificat are truly those who are the most despised among people, this will change everything. There can no longer be any pulling down of human beings for the greater glory of God. There can no longer be any vanity or any idolizing of human beings in the name of humanity. All that remains are human beings, brothers and sisters to love whoever they are, all human beings, partners in the struggle to exalt the lowly. Still the question remains: Who are the lowly and the hungry?"

It is always the same clearheadedness that goes side by side with trust. "Did people ever forgive Saint Francis for kissing the leper? What didn't people do to prevent Saint Francis de Sales or Saint Vincent de Paul from making us plunge too deeply into poverty? And what have we done to Saint Benedict Labre, who so madly loved the Son of God reduced to wretchedness? Why did he represent a unique specimen in and of himself? Why was the Church unable to make room for him?"

Perhaps even the Church will have a long road to travel. It will be one of suffering. "The Church will always experience the pangs of giving birth to justice, truth, and love. She will not be able to rest before extreme poverty is eradicated, before the poor are freed and saved. In the meantime, her whole body will go hungry; the table will remain empty as long as the only ones who matter — the downcast and excluded — are not there." This is how Father Joseph speaks to a group of Christians in 1973. He himself partakes in this suffering of a Church in the pangs of childbirth as much as in the suffering of the poor who are waiting for her. Yet trust would nonetheless prevail. In 1988, he has a last meeting with Volunteers who have formed a study group on spirituality.

"I am sure that some day the Lord will make a new community spring from the Volunteer Corps. It will not be a revolutionary community at all; it would really be pretentious to think so. It will rather be a community with a new sensitivity to Christ who died in utter wretchedness. We do not claim to be inventing something. It is enough that we allow ourselves to be used by the Lord so that He can invent a new form of spirituality...

"All of this rests on an intense life of prayer and contemplation of Christ, who was born, who lived, and who died in sheer wretchedness and who, over the centuries, continues to bear the stigma of human misery. It will be rooted in a fraternal community of people who pray within the overall fraternal community of volunteers... People who wish to be even less conspicuous, even more like servants than the others... The disciples at the hour of the washing of the feet... People who have only one passion: to experience with Jesus Christ the madness of love."

The Church, the place where I breathe; the Volunteer Corps, my family; areas of extreme poverty, places for worshipping Jesus Christ: there are still so many things left to understand. Has Father Joseph's history with his Church perhaps hardly begun?

## Chapter Fourteen

# "BECAUSE A GREAT LOVE CAN NEVER BE KEPT FOR ONESELF"

### "He died with us."

On February 16, 1988, some very poor families from the Parisian area meet again in the People's University.[22] Two days earlier, Father Joseph has returned to his Maker. He was still very much alive at Christmas, talking and singing with them. Pictures taken during this occasion show faces shining with joy despite the marks of deprivation, faces whose very transfiguration seems to justify all of Father Joseph's life. But on the evening of February 16, they are stunned. The families are trying to put their feelings into words. Mr. Russel remains silent for a long time, listening to the others. Then he picks up the microphone. "What I have been wanting to say for several minutes, what I am feeling, is that, since Monday, while at my work, my heart has been bleeding. I was in pain and, until our arrival here a little while ago, I was suffering so badly, and my heart was hurting me so much, that I did not know how to act. Tears were falling from my eyes uncontrollably. But what I felt with you just now is the love within this suffering. Here we are so close together that

22 People's Universities were created in Europe in the 1970s as places for training and exchanges between very poor families and those who agree to recognize them as partners. Father Joseph described them: "Crossroads between the experience of life of the underprivileged and that of other citizens, they are places for the creation of a new relationship between people." Since 1975, the People's Universities have been the starting point of the International Fourth World congresses, and it is from these universities that the delegations of representatives to national and international authorities are chosen.

we feel fine, we are ready for this suffering, we are even happy to suffer out of love for Father Joseph."

Starting with this first meeting after Father Joseph returned to God, tongues are becoming untied. Not all of them possess the same gift for expressing themselves as Mr. Russel, who knows how to put into words what others are thinking. Yet everyone has something intense to share.

*Father Joseph's last People's University in Paris, 1987.*

"He died with us," says a mother from Caen. And a man from Bordeaux adds: "He died for his ideal, but his ideal is all of us who are still alive, so his hope is still alive. Since he wanted us to continue carrying on with his work when he would be in the beyond. We are a sign, all of us who are here. He did not die in vain."

"All of us who are here ..." But how do these families know that Father Joseph gave his life to them? It is no longer only families who witnessed his life first-hand who come together in the People's University, at the Commemorative Stone on the Human Rights Plaza[23] and, especially, around his tomb at the foot of the chapel in the Hameau de Vaux. Men and women who have never seen him meet there too. Among them are households literally from nowhere, homeless, whose very existence is not recognized, just like the families of thirty-two years ago in the Camp of Noisy-le-Grand.

Let us remember: "Right from the start, the families forced me to acts of self-denial for which I would not have had the strength on

[23] The Commemorative Stone is the marble plaque placed on the Trocadero Plaza in Paris, where the Universal Declaration of Human Rights was signed in 1948. On October 17, 1987, in front of 100,000 people, Father Joseph Wresinski unveiled the Commemorative Stone. (See Chapter 12). October 17 was declared "World Day to Overcome Extreme Poverty" by the United Nations in 1992. On the 17th of each month, people in many countries gather for a short commemoration to honor people who suffer from extreme poverty and to renew their commitment to them.

my own. This is what happened to me for instance when a family landed in the Camp one day in February 1957, sent by the prefecture of Versailles. Two parents and five children arrived with no luggage and chilled to the bone. There was only one thing to do: give them my blankets. I thought that I would get some back the very next day or a little later. The situation did not get straightened out that easily and, in the middle of winter, I had to stay in a freezing shack with only my cassock and my cloak to cover myself with."

Who among his friends in Paris was aware of this? As for the families in the Camp, they ended up believing in the unbelievable: a priest who did not own anything because he gave away everything he had. That spoke volumes to them; but how were they to express what that meant to them? The outside world has not shared the knowledge and power of words with them. By what mysterious communion do Fourth World families manage to understand anyway, as if from the inside, this Father Joseph who belongs to them? How do they manage to talk about him among themselves? "I can't explain it; I do not have the words; these are things I feel ..." A Dutch Volunteer writes, "I went to Amsterdam to tell the families who have no telephone about the bad news. Mrs. S. broke down. She cried and cried. We just sat there, together. She did not express herself in words." One year later, Mrs. S. still does not find all the words that she would like to. "I do not know how to put it. But it is clear in my mind. Now that he is no longer with us, I have to speak up. I will come along on the pilgrimage to Rome. I do not know much about religion and the Pope. But I have got to go to Rome to talk about Father Joseph. This is his Church."

From now on, all the People's Universities will be involved in learning how to talk about Father Joseph. Taking part in these Universities, going to the Commemorative Stone on the Human Rights Plaza, and visiting Father Joseph's tomb in Méry-sur-Oise are separate activities; even if they are closely linked, the families tell them apart. In the Universities, they practice public speaking and develop a unique knowledge about something they will be the only ones to really understand. In fact, who could understand, as do the Fourth World families themselves, the choice Father Joseph made for them?

"He was born poor, and he died with us."

"He really saw things like we do. I liked what he said: 'Deepest poverty means you can never be sure of holding onto the ones you love.' That was his life: poverty, wretchedness. He knew it as a child, as a young man, and even when he grew older. It was his entire existence."

"He was a man who had lived in extreme poverty, but once he had escaped from it, he could have said, 'I am not going to worry about the poor any more.' He did escape from it; he became a priest; he reached a high-level position. He could have said, 'Now I am no longer in extreme poverty.' It was the exact opposite that happened. *He* always continued with the poor."

"When he became a priest, he could have asked for a quiet, trouble-free parish. But he went spontaneously toward the poorest, his brothers and sisters."

"When you realize that he had a trade as a pastry cook! Becoming a priest must really have been a choice... It makes people confident knowing that he lived in extreme poverty and all that. Even those who never met him."

A Volunteer writes from Montreal: "Raymond went to school for three years. Reading and writing is very difficult for him. But every evening he goes behind closed doors to read a page of *Blessed Are You the Poor!* He and a friend are discovering Father Joseph together. They recognize themselves in what he says about the very poor."

A man from Limburg also says, "He was among the poorest, but he had the courage to go see rich people to tell them what poverty was all about. Someone who goes to see rich people to talk to them about the poor is not well thought of... As for me, I would like to know how many times they turned him out of their homes, saying, 'What do you think you're doing coming to our homes to tell us your stories? What have we got to do with other people's poverty?' In the beginning, didn't they say that he was crazy? He really had courage as well as patient endurance. Can you picture me going to tell all that to wealthy people? I wouldn't even dare to think about it!"

**"Father Joseph did not take our place; he let us have our own."**

Less disadvantaged friends do not think first about Father Joseph's radical choice when he entered the seminary and then again when he arrived at the Camp of Noisy-le-Grand. Very disadvantaged families, though, seem to have always been aware of it. They have recognized the signs, and their lives have been changed by it. It continues to change their lives because Father Joseph's choice means that they, too, are committed. Just as they are committed because of the humility with which he lived in their midst. His presence alone would not have been enough to put them on their own feet if there had not been that flawless humility. Who better than these families could appreciate it?

"He often said that if he had been all alone, he could not have done what he did, and that it was thanks to us that he was able to go on. That was what he said, and he knew so well how to convey strength and courage to us."

"He also said that the mothers were women of courage, raising their children without any resources." How does this mother know? She joined the Movement after February 14, 1988. "I would have liked so much to know this man. I never met him. So now I take notes. I also took notes listening to the recording of the interview Father Joseph gave."

A father from Versailles continues, "Although he was the one who started the Movement, he said, 'The poor thrust themselves upon me.' That meant even though we may be wretched and depressed, no one will ever take away our pride... Our pride is not that of the rich. A rich man has all the pride of his wealth and success... *We* have natural love, the love that nature has given to human beings. Here is how I see altruism: it means pushing others onto center stage so that they can have their place in the sun. Father Joseph did not take our place; he let us have our own."

"He did not thrust his love on people; he waited for them to take it."

"He never thought of himself as a big shot."

"The honor and pride of poor people ran through all that he was, coming back like a prayer."

"He did not puff himself up with pride; he made us feel proud."

"As for me, I got to appreciate Father Joseph firsthand when the Pope came to Lyon. Only one of us could speak to him. Father Joseph took me by the arm: 'You are the one who is going to speak.' I said, 'No, this is something you have to do.' He answered me, '*I* am not the Movement. It is people like you, all of you, who have created the Movement. I had nothing to do with it.' So I was the one who introduced the Fourth World Movement to the Pope. Even though I was trapped in extreme poverty and no longer believed in God. It keeps crossing my mind; it's just wonderful. Father Joseph felt what the future holds. He knew that people who were so wretched could not stay that way. Look at all he brought me, not in terms of money, but better still: showing you that you are a human being, that you are capable, and that you must get out of this mess."

### "He thought like we do."

A man who matters so little in his own eyes can make other people matter and feel proud because of them. The families are the first ones to understand the text that Father Joseph left as a legacy to Christian families who participate by the thousands in the gatherings in Erpent in Belgium. The National Association of Parents, Alumni and Friends of After-School Clubs organizes these meetings annually. Father Joseph should have led the one that took place in March 1988. He was no longer there to do so. However, until the eve of his hospitalization, he prepared his text, always with the same sensitive concern for his audience. He would leave behind a meditation about the Holy Family that would be read at Erpent, and later published by the magazine *Direct* and the magazine of the French-speaking dioceses of Belgium, *La Foi et le Temps*. There are families who have trouble reading and whose rough-and-tumble lives do not incline to meditation. Still, are they not the first ones able to imagine the love that Father Joseph shared by living it himself and that he evoked at Erpent?

"This, then, is the ultimate self-denial, the self-denial that propels someone else ahead of us, that requires this tender outlook that makes this other person feel loved, respected, and carried forward. It requires this loving outlook that allows others in turn to commit themselves. What a blessing then, if the other person's commitment becomes my own, becomes by this very fact a common commitment! This approach is the very approach of the Christian family. It is also the approach of all men and women of goodwill who devote themselves completely to building a more humane world — a world where every human being becomes able to create love, to experience love, and to build a loving world.

"You see that we are dealing here with a concern that goes far beyond us, that encompasses all of mankind. We are dealing with coexistence in the fullest sense of the word, a coexistence that makes one continually aware of other people's presence, that prompts us to want them to succeed in creating love in their own right and in sharing it. Because a great love can never be kept for oneself."

The Erpent meditation sums up an entire life. It had to become a lifetime's experience before it could be written down. And it had to be experienced with the very poor so that it could become *their* meditation. Father Joseph knew they were capable of, and longing for, contemplation in an existence that did not offer them the right conditions for it.

Today, under the shock of separation, families are looking for words to express what they have contemplated in their hearts all through these years of sharing life and love with him. Earlier, the need for words had not been the same. Father Joseph was there; he was among them; that was the main thing. Now there is a sense of urgency. How can they make sure that they do not lose this man whom they have never had to mistrust?

"It never occurred to me that he might not be there," says a woman who has only known him for three years.

Others add: "He was the Father of the very poor; he tried to save us."

"He is first among the poor."

"He considered each one of us personally."

"He thought like we do; he understood. Every day he has known deepest poverty. He went where things were the worst. He knew..."

"He had experienced extreme poverty; he felt what we were going through. We did not need to put our lives on display, but it was all quite ordinary to him."

"He was our congressman, our representative."

"He told himself, 'I am a priest; I have to manage to save them.' That was where his roots were."

Mr. D., a Moslem migrant worker who, with his family, is experiencing considerable hardships, tells Bernadette Cornuau, "I turned his photo toward the sun, because Father Joseph could only

*Burkina Faso, 1986.*

be facing the sun. But since his photo was in danger of being damaged by the sun, I put it in a good spot with my family snapshots, because he is part of my family."

Eyewitness accounts also come from far away. From a town in Western Africa, Gabriel M., a former prisoner, writes, "I was courtyard supervisor. Sister Simone, our Volunteer, had talked to Father Joseph about me. I took him to visit the courtyard, but he immediately asked me to see the place where the most exhausted prisoners were. We went to holding room 6, in tier I, the place everyone was afraid to go into. Father Joseph went in. He went over to greet the sickest man, lying on a mat at the far end of the cell... He laid his hand on everyone who was sick. After the meeting with all the delegates, he came out under the tree to pray with all the prisoners, and he asked the guards to join us too."

Mucktar L. was there, too, that day. "The day Father Joseph came to the penal colony, he suffered a great deal in the infirmary. Right away he began to cry. That impressed me a lot. It was the first time that I saw a white person cry because of a black person. It upset me a lot."

In the penal colony, Father Joseph started a Knowledge Club. "When he came to the colony, he had a practical way of addressing us at the club. We were sitting down. He told us to hold hands, and he said, 'This is how you should take care of the least among you and not give up on one another.' I feel that anyone spending even a half hour talking with Father Joseph experiences more than just learning something; it is a real opportunity. Those thirty minutes were enough to enable me to take control of my life the rest of the time. He told us to 'never lose sight of that legacy of courage, even if you are in prison.'"

In the heart of an African-American neighborhood near New Orleans, a mother who had not been able to meet Father Joseph during his visits, tells a Volunteer, "It's funny, but it's as if it's Father Joseph who is talking to me, and I can talk to him. He understands me; he knows about our life; he knows what it means not to have any food on the table." Her neighbor adds, "How I would like to read his books! I would like to have known him." Another woman, each time she speaks about him, repeats, "He loved every adult, every child everywhere in the world. He taught us how to love people, all people."

## "Sent by God to Save People from All This Wretchedness"

Families are thinking more now about the fact that Father Joseph was a priest, sometimes wondering why he became one. "Did he do it for us? Was it to get support in fighting against extreme poverty more effectively?" In any event, the fact that he was a priest does make a difference. It made him the target of insults; he needed even more courage. "Trust me, they insulted him from head to foot. They gave him a hard time because of his cassock. They would mutter, 'Our priest is doing this; our priest is telling us that.' Still they were very happy to turn to him... He missed his calling as a traditional priest by choosing extreme poverty."

Then again: "If Father Joseph had not been a priest, would things really have been the same? As a priest, he got more recognition than we did. And since he was a priest, all people were his children."

" Since he was a priest, he understood the most underprivileged better. He was happy to be doing this work."

"Father Joseph was sent by God to save people from all this wretchedness. This was a gift that God had given him to promote all the poor as much as possible."

"Thanks to the love he had inside himself, just by looking at him, we felt cheered up."

"He talked like God would have talked; that helped us."

"I think that God put him on this earth with a plan in mind and not by accident."

Here is a conversation between two mothers. Mrs. H. is a Christian. "In my opinion, Father Joseph is the one who taught us, who formed the Fourth World to teach us to love one another and to help the families who are the poorest... What happened on the Trocadero Plaza was like the Gospel. There were the doctors of the law and the disciples. As for Father Joseph, he was speaking on behalf of the blind and the lame. He was speaking on behalf of his people." Mrs. B. is a Moslem. "Father Joseph said, 'Blessed are we the poor.' That means that if we are together — even if we are enduring great suffering — if we are together we are blessed, and that lightens the load. When people help one another, when we don't have enough to eat, for example, if we are together, we feel a little relieved anyway. It is in this sense that he means 'Blessed are we the poor.' That gives a lot of courage. If we are together, we can put together a great deal of courage... If each of us respects other people, our circle grows wider and wider, and, in my opinion, extreme poverty disappears. Because it is the Church that stands up for poor people's honor."

These are signs showing a communion that many friends experienced firsthand, without ever being able to understand or fathom it. The communion between a man who was intimately at home within the Gospels and families of all religious beliefs who say, "We are his people." It informs these simple words: "He thought like we do." How could such unity grow deeper during those years when the hardships and crises caused by chronic poverty did not prompt lofty speeches? All we know is that it grew, that it exists, and that it still calls for commitment on the part of the families.

*Father Joseph at a forum in Lille, France, 1983.*

In an album at the Ile-de-France People's University, families talk to him: "Father Joseph, thanks for having given all of us a warm welcome. You are warmly welcomed by all of us too."

"In my opinion, you aren't dead; you will always be in my heart."

"You are a major figure in our history... your struggle lives forever... you will live forever among outcasts like us."

Around the world, other families join in. "Father Joseph is not a man of the past. He is behind us, but he is in front of us too."

## Support the Poorest and Refuse Charity and Handouts

He is in front. Obviously, Father Joseph calls for commitment in times to come. How can we listen to these families without feeling our hearts ache? "Now it is up to us to do things the way Father Joseph did," says a man who joined the Movement after Father Joseph's death. And people close to him are constantly recalling all that this means.

"When you are trapped in extreme poverty, you are not living in the same world as other people. Father Joseph knew how to show us that we were just as important as other people"

"I should no longer live just for myself now, but for the poorest families; I should pass things on to them."

"When I consider all that he brought into my life, I don't have the right to give up on him. On the contrary, I ought to be with him even more, even though he is no longer here."

"As far as Father Joseph is concerned, what enables me to go on is that he gained recognition for the history of the Fourth World. Our history! Who else in society could do that? Who else could make the history of the poorest people known? As a young person from the Fourth World, how am I going to continue? It will be by putting into practice what Father Joseph started, by communicating his messages, by gaining recognition for our rights, and by always moving forward."

"He taught us to be in touch with the very poorest among families, to understand one another, to bear with one another, to live together. His path was mapped out. He had courage; we must follow his example. Whenever we think of him, we wonder: if Father Joseph were here, what would he say, what would he do? He should never be blotted out, and we should always follow his inspiration."

"He told us, 'You're big enough to fight your own battles. It is up to you to carry on and together to show other people that we are brave enough to manage anyway.' That's what Father Joseph wanted to show us — that we really had willpower. It is great that he is here to tell us that we have willpower. We were not always really in high spirits, but he was there to cheer us up. 'Go ahead, get started and you will see; afterwards, you will get results and reap rewards.' So that is why I'm saying to you, to all people who have trouble making both ends meet: It is up to you. You are brave; you are strong enough to get out of the mess that you are in. Friends are there to help you. You should not be caught alone in extreme poverty; you should not stay home behind closed doors. That is what Father Joseph meant."

In every country, adults, youths, and children keep coming back to the basics: getting along together, supporting the most despondent and, of course, refusing charity and hand-outs.

"He wanted us to get a guaranteed minimum income[24] rather than to have to go to soup kitchens. Because, when we go to soup kitchens, we really experience the most painful form of human misery. He wanted to do something else rather than seeing us line up to get a food package."

"*He* wanted us to have the same life as other people. Equality..."

"It is thanks to Father Joseph's fighting for it that we got the minimum income. But Father Joseph succeeded above all in drawing together poor people trapped in hardship so that they would stand up together — stand up together to ensure that human rights are respected."

"He was very demanding. He always wanted us to go farther, to see things through to the end. There was a real need for someone to wake us up; otherwise we would have sunk even deeper."

When they talk like this among themselves, families are turning their minds' eyes toward the Commemorative Stone on the Human Rights Plaza. The text engraved there and signed by Father Joseph proclaims the sacred duty of coming together to ensure that these rights are respected. Some parents read, "It is a sacred *right* to be able to defend one's children, one's neighbors, other people." In the opinion of the most underprivileged, "Struggling to eradicate extreme poverty is a sacred *right*." The duty they learned from Father Joseph is to do this together, to look constantly for people

---

24 Guaranteed minimum income, one of a whole series of integrated measures recommended for adoption by the French government in the Wresinski Report. As a comprehensive policy to eliminate chronic poverty, it proposed that every adult living in France whose income fell below the poverty level should automatically receive a monthly guaranteed minimum wage regardless of any previously existing conditions.

poorer than themselves, and to go toward "people who are too miserable to come to the Commemorative Stone." The families realize they must continue — but continue with others, with those whom they do not know yet, "because they are hidden; they are homeless; they are hiding in the woods." We have to share pride in the Commemorative Stone with them.

"The Commemorative Stone means that we are defending our rights. As far as I am concerned, I feel proud each time I go there."

"As for me, when I go there, it gives us strength. We are living in a trailer, and soon we will have to move. But when we go to the Commemorative Stone, we feel very proud. And I ask everyone who is here to go there often, because it really makes you feel better."

Pride and relief are also felt by people who have lost loved ones in conditions of extreme poverty. Many have not received a decent burial. Who has acknowledged that they were victims of extreme poverty even in death? A wife, pointing out the Commemorative Stone, says, "My husband is there."

## A Legacy to Embrace

So few words are available to express such momentous things. A mother who came from Amsterdam to attend the funeral mass on February 18, 1988, like many others, could only cry. One year later, she summarizes her commitment like this: "His life and his suffering are valuable to mankind. Now he ought to rest. I would like people to leave him alone. ***He*** is up there close to God, doing everything he should be doing. But down here, it is up to us to continue now... During his lifetime, Father Joseph built something like a large workshop. It was not like those old factories in my neighborhood, but a beautiful, large, modern workshop, very well lit. And he put benches and chairs everywhere. It is our duty to fill them up. *I* am going to help the lady across the street to pay for her fare to the People's University. I do not have any money either, but I am going to manage to find those sixteen guilders." At the People's University in Wijhe on June 17, 1989, with other mothers, she again asserts, "Just like we counted on him, Father Joseph can count on us now." She belongs to a Protestant Church group in her neighborhood, but, because of Father Joseph, she has decided to take part in the Fourth World families' pilgrimage to Rome. All participants sense a new responsibility; and how can we listen to them without an aching heart? What means indeed does society offer to enable them to shoulder responsibility for their struggle? The man who knew so well how to change people's hearts is no longer standing beside them.

*Cardinal Lustiger celebrates a funeral mass for Father Joseph in the Cathedral of Notre-Dame of Paris on February 18, 1988.*

Marie Jahrling, who pulled through the ordeal of the Camp of Noisy-le-Grand with the calm dignity that her mother already embodied, bears witness during a meeting in Paris: "Father Joseph had told us about the importance of the cornerstone in holding a building up. Today I want to say that the cornerstone, the heart, has fallen to pieces. But, as workers in the building trade would say, *we* are going to make sure that the cement is so strong that the building will never, ever collapse." Her brother-in-law, Bernard Jahrling, longtime companion of Father Joseph, puts it this way: "What hope lies in being able to tell the world about the road Father Joseph traveled with the poorest; in being able to say that he offered this path that is love and that other men and women followed it! He has given hope to all those men, women, and children who do not know the meaning of the words, 'I am going to eat.' On this February 14, 1989, I am thinking about the Fourth World and that no one is lonely any longer. Thank you, Father Joseph." Bernard followed Father Joseph from the Camp of Noisy-le-Grand to Pierrelaye, and then to Méry-sur-Oise. Together, they built or renovated countless walls and houses. In his opinion, the life of his companion and guide is crystal clear — there is nothing to add or to take away. People have to follow him now, and Bernard knows far too much about chronic poverty not to realize that this will not be easy. For where will they go? What will they do? On whom can they count?

A father from Rennes raises the question that is essential in the eyes of all the families when speaking about the October 17 ceremony around the Commemorative Stone. "There were a lot of organizations there... It was important to see so many public figures. But people, public figures must keep their promises now." A friend answers him, "If people carry out what is written on the Commemorative Stone, there will be more justice. This is really Father Joseph's idea: To put an end to extreme poverty. But that is not going to happen overnight. We have to persuade people to join us." But who will do the persuading now? Another man says, "It seems to me that a century will perhaps not be long enough to find another man of such stature."

Mr. Russel, who was so affected by the shock of Father Joseph's death in February 1988, also discloses to us a year later how vast the legacy to embrace appears to him. "Father Joseph said, 'The search for the poor is always going on somewhere in the Church.' To dive to the bottom and to experience incarnation among the very poor were the reasons why he became a priest. To search for God among the poor... Besides, people are not often aware of that. People know Father Joseph as the founder of the Fourth World Movement, but not as a priest.

"When one looks at the core of his personality, he was a man of infinite goodness. I have always said that he ought to be canonized. Caring deeply about other people's hardships means going straight to Jesus Christ. This was how he carried out his faith and how he fulfilled his role as a priest. He taught human beings how to love one another. His life shows me that it is possible to gather together people who are different — believers or atheists — in order to find the same love that is needed to eradicate human misery, to listen to one another, to stop treating one another heartlessly, no longer thinking 'It's their fault; they handled things badly...'

"He pointed out the inner consistency of chronic poverty. He explained, but not by saying, 'The rich are to blame.' No; on the contrary, he said, 'It is through love that we will succeed in eradicating the extreme poverty that human beings have been foolish enough to create.' Father Joseph experienced poverty when he was a child. He knew what people who have suffered feel in their heart of hearts. He did not idealize them; he shared in their very being...

And he always saw love as the means to destroy extreme poverty. It is not like it was in 1789, it is not a question of rebellion. It is a matter of joining together, a question of a revolution of the heart."

Mr. Russel also speaks about the Wresinski Report[25] and human rights. "This is not a plan that can be shortened or reduced to a package of band-aids. All of it must be applied to eradicate human misery. For this plan aims to end extreme poverty and not to distribute relief. Putting an end to extreme poverty means granting people rights. We should not have to beg for them; we should get them as a birthright, simply because we have come into this world. But, in this case, our struggle has to be all the more determined. We cannot wait for our rights to be delivered like flowers or a gift."

A revolution of the heart, a determined struggle... But then who can they count on, now that Father Joseph is no longer around to galvanize people of goodwill and courage, to always recognize potential victories as well as those we will have to wait for? Could it be that these families feel they can still count on him? In 1989, we must accept the evidence. The tomb in the Hameau de Vaux in Méry-sur-Oise has become a place of pilgrimage for people from all walks of life and of all creeds. The infinite care and patience that Father Joseph brought to renovating the grounds and facilities of the former convent and to building a new chapel there have taken on an unexpected meaning. He wanted this place to be like a home for the Volunteer Corps which, even after spreading to the four corners of the earth, had nothing to call its own. He had asked that, when the time came, his final resting place be at the foot of the chapel. On August 2, 1988, the Volunteer Corps brought him back home, and his tomb has become what he himself always was as a person: a place for gathering; a place for facing certain basic truths about humanity and about God; a place from which one returns to daily life feeling refreshed, stimulated, and determined to move ahead. To go there, one does not need to be a believer in any specific way. "We believe in love," and "Father Joseph belongs to everyone."

---

[25] The Wresinski Report was widely adopted as the name for *Chronic Poverty and Lack of Basic Security*, Father Joseph Wresinski's report to the French Economic and Social Council. (See Chapter 12.)

Even in front of his tomb, families express themselves sparingly.

"Father Joseph has gone, but he is still with us. He was the Father of poor people from every country."

"He did not want to see people in poverty. I do not want Father Joseph to be forgotten, nor his tomb to be forgotten. I would like him to be known around the world. His heart was filled with other people's wretchedness."

"Still nothing is lost; that is what matters. In spite of the fact that he is no longer here, he left his presence."

"Father Joseph, I thank you for all the love you have given to us. Thanks to you, we can walk with our heads held high. You gave honor back to all the poor people in the world. You have not died, since you will stay in our hearts forever to summon us to fight with ever-increasing strength."

"Father Joseph, do not let us get into the habit of slacking off. You and the Volunteers together, you have loads of courage, and on your burial site we can engrave the words, 'Welcome, Hope, Light, and Joy.'"

*The chapel in Méry-sur-Oise, France, where Father Joseph was laid to rest. 1989.*

A whole group of families from Reims comes to pray beside his grave. Whatever their beliefs, they all talk to Father Joseph. Then they decide to write down their remarks to leave them with him. "We had arrived in Pierrelaye feeling discouraged and ready to throw in the towel. After having seen and heard you, we left for Reims with the determination to continue our struggle, and I thank you for that. You made us stand up on our own feet and, whatever may happen, the people of the Fourth World will go on standing up straight. We promise you this."

This is how families string their words together like beads one after the other:

"As you told us; 'Wherever extreme poverty exists, human rights are violated.' I want to ask you to give us the strength to go out and reach the very poorest."

"My only regret in life is never having known you."

"We should not forget that Father Joseph was very kind-hearted to the whole world. This is something that we will never forget. I pray close to him, and so does my family."

"As you well know, what we are asking for is dignity, pride, and that our children also go on fighting, so that some day there will be no more injustice, so that things change at last. Life is about sharing, not about being selfish! You understood so well, Father Joseph, that what we families want is not to have to beg, but rather to be able to manage on our own."

"Together we have learned how to remain a people standing tall, thanks to you, Father Joseph. You knew so well how to make us understand the meaning of sharing, of friendship and, above all, of respect toward the most underprivileged."

Around Father Joseph's tomb, his long-standing dream for the families seems to be coming true: the realization that human misery is a "voucher" in front of the world and before God. It is also as a "voucher" that they offer him their sorrow, that they are no longer saying that he experienced their extreme poverty, but rather that they experienced his.

"I have gone through the same grinding poverty as Father Joseph. People should never lose hope. I was able to get my children back after being separated from them for ten years... I am enduring the same terrible poverty as you, and many people are enduring it. You gave me the strength to go on living. Even when you are living in poverty, there are always people worse off than you are."

"Going to Méry is a pilgrimage," Mr. Pioline from Rennes concludes very plainly. Then Mrs. Chatton adds, "Now it is a rallying point, because it is a place where we go together with all the family, and we can go back there every year."

## Families and Volunteers: A New Alliance

Turning to Father Joseph and asking him for guidance and support also means visiting the place where Volunteers meet and train together, and from which they set out again into the world — those Volunteers whose grief the families were the first to understand. Because it was men and women from areas of extreme poverty who instantly felt the sorrow in the hearts of Volunteers, who could not put it into words either. One mother, after the funeral mass, kept on repeating the same words, "This is rough; this is hard on us." Suddenly she looked at us and said, "But maybe it is even harder for you Volunteers. You used to follow him everywhere." As time goes by, something like a new communion, a new tenderness is springing up between families and Volunteers. Is this perhaps the start of a new outlook on the part of families?

"I was looking around recently when we went to Méry-sur-Oise, when we saw all those young people who were leaving their families and all to go to Guatemala, or anywhere else for that matter. These youths have promising professions, and they are leaving everything to go help others. Well, we owe it all to Father Joseph anyway."

A father from French-speaking Switzerland expresses his faith in the future. "Father Joseph has deserved a rest now, and he put his trust in the Volunteers. Volunteers know that if they do not move ahead on the road he mapped out, he will start spinning in his grave." A man from Lille feels the same way. "Father Joseph stood for perfection. He wanted to take time; he wanted things to be attractive, even places where Volunteers were living... What is nice is that there are new Volunteers. We still see the veterans like Jean-Luc Penet and the others. We see that they are staying faithfully in the same positions; there is always someone to represent the Movement, but there are new people as well."

As for these new Volunteers, no less than forty-two have arrived in the year following Father Joseph's passing away. But these men, women, and youths who have come because of him are facing a new responsibility that they do not yet measure. One day long ago, Father Joseph had spoken about the vulnerability of the first Volunteers working beside him in the Camp of Noisy-le-Grand. That same vulnerability had been the very foundation for the communion between Volunteers and families. He wondered then if that communion was not in danger of disappearing progressively as the Volunteer Corps grew and forged itself an identity in the world's eyes. However, he foresaw that a time would come when this frailty would once again be deeply felt. In his opinion, this was essential, because a Volunteer Corps that was sure of itself would be unbearable to the very poor. But he was deeply worried by this as well: "Are they going to last and, if they last, are they going to suffer?"

In 1986, he would pay a visit to the person whose friendship has never failed, especially not in the most difficult years: Father Léon Bach. One day, thirty years earlier, he had come to ask him, "What should I do; should I stay in the forlorn countryside of the Aisne?" In those days, Father Bach had known the answer: "You should not stay there." Thirty years later, wasn't it the same question that Father Joseph came to ask him? "Did I do it right? Can what I have built last?" Father Bach recounts, "He said that here at my table. He was really worried. 'Will there be someone to carry on with what I started?'" But this time, his friend no longer has the answer. "I could not answer that question. It was his life's work and his life's work had expanded worldwide. So I said, 'We have to hope it will continue.' We did not discuss it further. He wanted to see the church..."

Quite likely, in Father Joseph's opinion, when all is said and done, doesn't the answer lie in God's hands? But it also lies in the hands of the Volunteers and the families. He knew from the very beginning that he was entrusting to them the outcome of his life. They have begun to discover this after he returned to his Maker. These families are discovering how much he wanted a completely trustworthy Volunteer Corps to stand by them in a world that has not yet learned how to keep its promises to the poor. Do they realize how much they are speaking in his name when they remind Volunteers that they must ensure that Father Joseph's work is carried on? For these families, who consider themselves more responsible than ever before, also tell Volunteers, "Now it is up to you to see to it that things continue."

So around the tomb in Méry-sur-Oise, families and Volunteers are becoming aware of the common legacy to shoulder. This legacy, which will make them strong while keeping

*Father Joseph's tomb, 1989.*

them vulnerable, is to remain faithful to the poorest of the poor. "He used to say, 'You are right here, but there must be others farther on. Aren't there poor people perhaps in places where we have not gone yet?' Father Joseph was demanding; he always urged us to take one extra step." Father Joseph also entrusted Volunteers with this mission of giving priority to families in poverty who have not yet been identified. On the evening before his operation, he reminds them one last time, "Our vocation is to stay very, very close to the most disadvantaged among the families. I must remind you of this, because we will always be tempted to lean on the most dynamic, most courageous, and most intelligent families. Of course we have to lean on them, but we cannot let ourselves be monopolized and hemmed in by them. We cannot allow them to come between us and the very poorest."

The mission, then, is a common one, nurturing unity and strength, if it is true that the suffering of the very poor is the ultimate weapon against all of humanity's selfishness. Families and Volunteers are shouldering a common mission. Still, Father Joseph, don't you think that you are sending out around the world a very fragile crew? But then again, would you, who loved the families so much, have called them up to this struggle if it could not be won?

## Chapter Fifteen

# HE CHANGED THE WORLD'S OUTLOOK

### The World Also Bears Witness

"Out of his childhood of wretchedness, out of his life in the midst of outcasts, he brought forth a history, a sociology, a driving force for action, a comprehensive policy and a spirituality. A pragmatic man, he rallied around himself hundreds of full-time volunteer workers, and tens of thousands of supporters; he knew how to catch the ears of government leaders, of kings, of members of parliamentary bodies. He heightened the awareness of our age, blazing a new trail, and enabling us to hear something that, without him, we would never have heard: the voice of a people in deepest poverty.

"There remains, unending, the conversion of our souls. Therefore we must pore over his books and meditations, so carefully prepared, so powerful... Then we shall better understand what may sometimes have surprised or even offended us in his hard-hitting, uncompromising, and sober style when, suddenly, his words became those of a champion sharpshooter, firing with each round on mediocrity that deserves to be blown to pieces.

"For this reason and for the sake of God, Father Joseph risked his life, his whole life, the height and the breadth of it, in a tragic and unforgettable striving, in a frightening lesson of absolute thoroughness in the service of the most awesome of causes — that of the least among men and the first with God."

These words of Georges-Paul Cuny were published in the April 1988 issue of *Panorama Magazine.* He is a member of the Saint-

Francis-Xavier Parish in Paris. His article is like an answer across time to the Lenten sermons that Father Joseph preached in 1985 in this community that could be considered a world apart from an extremely poor one. Father Joseph spent his nights preparing his homilies. Each time on Saturday evenings and Sunday mornings, he left for Paris, his heart filled with anxiety. How, in this very orderly parish, should he talk about the disorder and despair of chronic poverty? How should he tell these unquestionably honorable families about the struggle for honor waged by families held in contempt? How should he talk about the preferential love of Jesus Christ for the very poor without making the rich doubt that they, too, were saved? Jesus spoke boldly to the rich young man. The latter went away sad and gloomy. How could he bring joy to the Saint-Francis-Xavier Parish?

During this 1985 Lenten season, Father Joseph lived once again inside the Gospels: the moments of rejoicing (Zacheus, come down from your tree; I need you); the unbelief of the learned; the weariness caused by ears that seemed to remain shut. At age sixty-seven, Father Joseph would not give up on trust. He could not; it was part of his personality. He would even allow his meditations to be published for the first time as a book: *The Poor, Meeting with the True God*. This title, it should be noted, was not chosen by him. In his opinion, there was not one God who was truer than any other: there was God. Still, for the first time in his life, he agreed to let his homilies be published. Yet, after preaching Lenten sermons in the heart of Paris, he came home with the same anxiety as usual: how does one convince people who own riches that stripping themselves of their possessions is a source of freedom and joy? All through the last years of his life, he would continue to bear the suffering of the poor waiting for humanity to change its heart. He also continued to bear the suffering of this same humanity, which has everything to offer the poor but which does not dare to make the decisive move. One Saturday night during this Lenten season, while driving back home to the Hameau de Vaux, Father Joseph told the Volunteers accompanying him, "It isn't over; we must always be ready to go up to Jerusalem."

Three years later, Georges-Paul Cuny replies, "Father Joseph has left. Suddenly. Mission accomplished." Then he adds, "There remains, unending, the conversion of our souls." What remains, indeed, is the question that was raised by Father Joseph and that his life continues to raise for us, the one raised by the very poor who frighten us and who ask us, "Do you believe that we are human beings? Do you believe in our suffering as human beings? Do you want us as brothers and sisters, as partners?"

In February 1988, many friends have begun to write. Testimonies from everywhere start pouring into Méry-sur-Oise. More and more people bearing witness are finding their way to the tomb in the Hameau de Vaux, this same path that Fourth World families have been the first to discover. They all remember crucial moments of Father Joseph's life, when he made truth ring out: the major international events at the *Mutualité* in Paris, at *Forest National* in Brussels, on October 17 around the Commemorative Stone on the Trocadero Plaza, or the adoption of the Wresinski Report. But this is not the main point. Just like the families, friends from all walks of life have in mind the person whose irresistible love and astonishing confidence, whose optimism and daring have stirred them deeply. In one way or another, they have all been disturbed by him, and this is what they remember. They recall what they learned from him.

Geneviève de Gaulle says, "So thirty years will have been long enough for you to entrust to our hands this Movement, conceived in the heart of a small child trapped in poverty. What you wanted to teach us is what you had learned yourself in times of grinding poverty and humiliation with your mother: the dignity of each human being and, first of all, of the most deprived and rejected among people, those whom God considers with special tenderness."

French political figures follow suit with words that are not exactly those of everyday political life:

"Father Joseph, nothing will ever be the same after you and thanks to you. You upset everything, stirred everything up, turned everything upside down."

"I would have liked to bear witness to the respect and the friendship that I felt for this apostle of the Gospel and of human rights, who, long before the problem became the focal point of political debates, devoted his life to relieving the suffering of the poor and the dispossessed."

"I was struck by the courage and determination with which he fought for all the disadvantaged. His life's work was based on love and altruism, but also on truth."

"May his memory continue insistently to challenge and to inspire us to more justice and generosity, as did the shining example of his life's actions."

Messages also pour in from international organizations and from friends around the world:

"By becoming the servant of the poor, Father Joseph Wresinski showed us the enormous task that someone who devoted his entire life to loving his fellow human beings could accomplish."

"To those who were fortunate enough to know him, his life, his dedication and his love will always inspire us."

*Pierrelaye, France, 1981. Father Joseph welcomes participants to the Seminar on "Extreme Poverty and Exclusion in Africa." "We had experienced such loneliness for a long time that we promised one another to look for people who, like you, are facing extreme poverty by themselves."*

"We supporters have also been very fortunate to know him well and to enrich ourselves with his way of thinking and the things he said, so that our lives can never again be hemmed in behind narrow and meaningless boundaries. Father Joseph enabled us to refocus our lives, which had been scattered and pulled apart by a myriad of demands and needs."

"I am moved by the memory of our meetings about extreme poverty in Africa. Father Joseph Wresinski knew how to listen to us Africans and how to carry on a dialogue with us about giving and receiving."

"I suffered so much when I heard about Father Joseph's death. He was the father of the world's poor people, white and black... He saw the suffering of poor people, and he devoted his whole life to making them happy."

"Apostle of the most underprivileged on the planet, Father Joseph, in my eyes, did not die. Every human being comes into this world to carry out certain tasks. When this person has finished the tasks and goes back home, people here below say he has died, whereas, in fact, he has gone back home."

It is not only the French head of state, the King of Belgium, the Secretary General of the United Nations, a top-level official of the Organization of African Unity, or an Ambassador of the Philippines or of Colombia who are speaking and writing. There are also hundreds of ordinary citizens: Salome Muigai, a school teacher in Kenya; Julio Javier Espindola, a doctor in La Paz, Bolivia; the mayor of San Jacinto, a small village in Guatemala; and even a prisoner in a detention center somewhere south of the Sahara; not to mention this group of convicts who tell a Volunteer, "All your brothers from the little community in Building C send you their condolences. To those of us who have believed in Jesus, Father Joseph is a real asset for the future." Whether a minister, a prominent civil servant, a teacher, or a convict, all of them, when considering Father Joseph, seem to have to look for the right words, much as Fourth World families do. All are gradually going to discover how words remain inadequate. "Father Joseph represents much more than himself as a person," says a supporter. "I mean that, usually, when you meet someone, you meet him with his personality and responsibilities. I have the feeling, maybe even more since he is no longer here, that when you met Father Joseph, you were meeting much more than merely himself as a person. You were even meeting more than the secretary general of ATD Fourth World. You were meeting someone a little like a representative of the human race, like a bearer of something universal." Friends will need time to understand what they

*Guatemala, 1985.*

have not yet grasped. Just like families will need time to put into words what they have understood from the very beginning.

### "He Charted a Course for the Church"

Will the Church also need time? This Church, that he loved, served, defended and, sometimes, disturbed, is beginning, in turn, to speak up. "I can say that it was one of the finest hours in the history of Notre-Dame of Paris, perhaps the finest one... I have never seen Notre-Dame look so beautiful, so alive and so transparent as on the day of Father Joseph's funeral. It was indeed wonderfully radiant with the love of Christ for the poorest, for the least... I have never given communion in such conditions: to so many blackened hands, to so many faces creased by life's pain and hardship."

This is how Father Hardy, Bishop of Beauvais, bears witness to the fact that, when Father Joseph returned to God, he had kept his promise. He had given the very poor back to our churches and cathedrals: Notre-Dame of Paris, Saint-Nicolas of Fribourg, Sainte-Bernadette of Port-au-Prince, Saint-Maurice of Angers. From Cardinal Lustiger to the humble brother in the bush, between Paris, Geneva and Bangui, between Guatemala City and some forgotten Amerindian villages in Peru, the Church acknowledges her servant: "Jesus identifies with the very poorest and the most disadvantaged. This is clear, simple and terrifying... To Father Joseph's mind, there was not a bit of the 'cult of suffering,' nor of sentimentalism, in all of this. It was as a priest that he was sent to Noisy-le-Grand, as a Christian that he wrote his books... As a true Christian, he was careful not to exalt the poor to the detriment of the wealthy, not to despise the wealthy whom Jesus loves, even if, to the hardhearted wealthy, he can only announce their downfall. Father Joseph reminded us, 'God does not lead partisan struggles,' Jesus told Nicodemus, 'No one should perish. But it is not enough for you to believe in me, Nicodemus, you also have to become a new man, leading a new life. Because God needs you.'"

"Joseph is a sign of the humiliated Christ who gives back to humiliated people an awareness of their dignity... His life was a constant gift of himself; it embodied the law of the grain of wheat that falls to earth to die in order to bear much fruit. I am sure that in the logic of God's love, his initiatives will not ring out in hollow emptiness, but that they have been of the quality that breathe life and set into motion a movement that will stretch beyond the present times... A shock wave has unfurled that has reached many people. And a door has also been opened onto the unseen. That really called forth my prayers and those of the sisters here... The Lord guided me to a small seminary in Benin; I can say that Father Joseph will remain in my memory and in my life. Is he not even closer to each of us now? Who else was able to say to a head of state, 'What about the poor?' Who else besides Father Joseph will still be able to say that? This is the Movement's future... During this mass, we are going to praise God and to pray that Father Joseph, who followed God's path on earth and who entered into God's glory, may entrust our people and all the very poor to our Father... God's grace filled Father Joseph; I thank the good Lord for that. Father Joseph welcomed this grace in the bottom of his heart, and he let it sink in deeper and deeper. He was not satisfied to let this grace work in his own heart; he put it to work in the heart of all those whom he met... Father Joseph charted a course for the Church. People can only believe in the Church if they follow the paths that Father Joseph took."

These are the words of Bishop Ligonde of Port-au-Prince in Haiti. In these forceful and clear terms, he speaks about the personality and the life of Father Joseph to the poor of Sainte-Bernadette Parish. Yet the Church will also need time to reach full understanding and to give back to the very poor the priest whom they, themselves, have given to her. Could anyone imagine that the Church would not take time for meditation and for prayer? For is there any greater justice to restore, any more wonderful promise of salvation to hold out than to give back to her despised people this priest who will intercede forever with God on their behalf? Does the Church not own an asset, which no secular institution could match, to be returned to the very poor?

## "I Am Making a Life-Long Commitment."

In the meantime, no one needs to wait for full understanding before making a commitment. Here, too, friends act like the families, regardless of beliefs. They are showing that we can follow with confidence a man whose life was crystal clear and persuasive, knowing that we will meet with insight for our own lives as we move ahead. Is this not what each person is saying in his or her own way?

"In reply to your letter of May 13, 1988, that informed me of the death of our sorely missed Father Joseph, who was loved by everyone in the Movement because of his fine character and his generosity, I ask full forgiveness for my delay in answering because of farm work in the fields. I am making a life-long commitment particularly to the Fourth World Movement... I will never forget Father Joseph."

From grueling farm work in the fields on the edge of the Sahel, to the highest levels of decision making in Europe, inside the Church and among ordinary citizens, people are making promises to the most disadvantaged:

"By continuing the work that was dear to his heart, we will enable him to abide with us."

"In our minds, he will always be the epitome of tireless compassion and active kindness."

"He will leave a lasting foundation in our consciences."

"The best homage that we can pay to him is to continue his work with renewed determination."

"The struggle of the very poor actively participating in the ATD Fourth World Movement must continue, and I shall stand beside them."

"I assure you that I shall stay close to you and to the work of the man who returned to God. I promise you my wholehearted interest and my undivided attention."

Familiar supporters, some of them retired people, make us feel as close to Father Joseph as ever.

"How does one speak about Father Joseph? When I think about all the time I shared with him, I see him again seated in our midst during our training sessions, our meetings, confiding his concerns to us, clarifying his thinking, conveying his hopes to us through all those whom he met around the world; listening to us too, reacting sometimes to encourage us, sometimes to calm our troubled spirits... When I recall the time I spent with Father Joseph, I remember having prayed the Salve Regina with him, having listened to him comment on texts of the daily masses, and having learned to understand that his priesthood was inseparable from his whole being. When I evoke the time I shared with Father Joseph, it includes bearing witness to the respect, the trust, and the hope that Fourth World families placed in the man who spoke to them frankly, precisely, as a way of respecting them better... For the future, I will keep in mind the fact that Father Joseph was a man with a way of thinking for our time that gives meaning to our lives and our world. Thanks to these memories that we have to nurture, we must feel the constant forward thrust needed so that the dignity of the very poor be recognized at last. For we are well aware that 'the struggle is never over' and that the task requires love and faithfulness."

Still another example of commitment comes to us from this young man of the Fond des Nègres hamlet in Haiti. "Today, Father Joseph is no longer with us, but we notice that his work is spreading and that, each time efforts are made, Father Joseph is there in our midst. Father Joseph made me love poor people. Father Joseph, you are a father; because of the spirit that you put in our hearts, you have become our adoptive father. This is true in the same way that Saint Joseph was Jesus' adoptive father. We are going to walk on, even if the road is sometimes a hard one. We climb the foothills, even if we do not find a place to sleep, even if we do not find what we want to eat. This commitment means that we are determined to help the very poor, without seeking to get any reward."

Finally, isn't this perhaps a commitment also on the part of this young couple from Limoges? "Since this summer, I have been rereading Father Joseph's four books while praying for him. Now that I feel his presence, his very vivid texts take on new life. I think that one of his wishes should be fulfilled: there ought to be contemplative sisters in Méry embodying a presence to God in communion with the very poor, extending hospitality of this quality to people who come to the Hameau de Vaux and to Pierrelaye."

A Volunteer, considering this outpouring of testimonies, recollections, and promises, comments, "When I imagine where Father Joseph was in the early years, in the mud of the Camp of Noisy-le-Grand... Only a great love could accomplish this miracle of changing the world's outlook." Father Joseph would probably agree with him in his own way. In his opinion, a great love for all mankind had already accomplished this miracle two thousand years ago. All anyone had to do, regardless of condition or creed, was put out into deep water to remind the world about it. Did he not say as much when talking about his early years of priesthood? "We believed — and I still believe — that the evangelization of the very poor had already been achieved." Born in dire poverty, he could be sure of what many believers do not seem to dare to trust in; namely, the genuine presence of Jesus Christ among the most abandoned of the earth.

## A Child's Outlook

Did he do anything else, in all those years, but to attempt simply and patiently to share with the world his own way of looking at things as a child? "As for me, I really had to start my journey through life from where I was born, with the experiences and the outlook that extreme poverty had given to me... Born in extreme poverty, I learned to see the world and my Church from the bottom."

"From the bottom," as did the little boy running along Brault Street to take the family goat to graze in the low-lying meadows. He was four years old then, and he saw the world from inside an old blacksmith's shop turned into lodgings for poor families. Having lost a daughter through lack of medical care, his mother had decided that this would never happen again. When her second daughter was born, she got her husband to agree to this extravagant expenditure: a goat to provide milk! By the time he was four, Joseph had already learned it all: reliance on assistance from other people that maintains neither one's dignity nor even one's body and soul; the exploits that the very poor are capable of in order to reject their inhuman condition; all their knowledge about life and God that is scorned and ignored. "The Holy Spirit dwells in them, too. They, too, are able to act for the well-being of others. They, too, are builders of humanity." All his life, Father Joseph would remind us of this. All his life, whenever he met people straining to "educate the poor," he would also think about his mother, a most intelligent and dignified lady among her peers, to whom ladies in charge of the parish's charities felt they had to teach the facts of life. Later on, mothers of Fourth World families would sense intuitively, "His mother taught him everything; she was brave, he held her in high esteem. He loved his mother a lot; he understood what she had gone through for her children. It is because of her that he went so far."

The outlook that changed the world's outlook was one forged by a child also learning from his mother indulgence for wealthy people who do not know what they are doing. This is the outlook of a child learning what faith in God can be when there is nothing more to expect from human beings. This child's outlook merely grew broader and sharper over the years, without ever becoming the outlook of a disillusioned adult who would have understood everything, judged everything, and condemned the world. The very poor cannot live without looking through the eyes of a child, ready to believe and forgive everything. If they condemned the world, would it not mean condemning their own hope first of all? This, too, is something that Father Joseph taught us. There is nothing astonishing in the fact that rich and poor children swarmed around him at all times. They recognized the eyes of the urchin from Saint-Jacques Street and, as far as he was concerned, Father Joseph knew what he was doing when he created the Tapori Movement with them. He knew what he was saying when he called them "champions of happiness." Children too, after February 14, 1988, write about their sorrow, looking for the right words.

"Father Joseph, you wanted an end to extreme poverty. You made us understand that we had to join together so that everyone could be joyful. Even though you have left us, we will not stop fighting, with all the Tapori members, so that everyone can be happy. You are historic, and I like you. Adrien."

"In the beginning, there were not many people to help him work with poor people so they could learn to read. But now, a lot of people are trying to carry on his work. Today, I want his name to be written in the dictionary so that people who live a hundred years from now will recognize that he was a fine person."

"I would like to thank him for having created the ATD Fourth World and the Tapori Movement. It allowed me to meet people from ATD who are struggling against everything that's unfair."

"I know that you continue to pray to God for us."

"Father Joseph paid attention to children, and, even though he is 'dead', he is thinking about us. Let us pray so that we do not forget him and so that we think about children who are not fortunate enough to be as lucky as we are. Let's love children the way Father Joseph did."

Children who never met him are also expressing themselves.

"I never knew you, but I liked you."

" I would have liked to know him. I hope that the ATD Fourth World Movement will continue its work like Father Joseph started it, because everyone is the same and no one is different."

"He loved all the children in the world, and he searched for happiness for everyone. He will remain in the hearts of all children who want to do something against everything that's unfair. He was one of those people who understood that all children are alike and that they have to come together to be stronger and happier."

*With children in Reunion Island, 1981.*

One young Muslim boy adds, "I don't know if my letter has gotten across well enough all the qualities needed to define Father Joseph's generosity, but I do know that we all love him... It is not because our Father Joseph has passed away that his friendship with children has passed away as well... Don't ever forget this friendship, and the good that he did to us children. I'd like to thank him a lot. Thanks, Father Joseph; good-bye, and see you soon."

In the children's opinion, it is obvious that Father Joseph now has to be taken as a model.

"To me, you were like Jesus; you helped poor people to live longer and better."

"Now we are going to act like you. It was great when you were with us. Good-bye, Father Joseph."

"I liked Father Joseph, because he liked everyone a lot. I think that it is because he loved Jesus."

"Thanks to you, Father Joseph, there are children who do not want extreme poverty. They want happiness."

"Father Joseph, you did a lot for us children, so now it is our turn to do something. Father Joseph is a rare kind of human being; he takes care of all those who crave love and affection. He is a person who thought about us children. He takes hatred out of our hearts. He is love in person. He brings children of all colors together."

And little Emmanuelle writes on a nice sheet of white paper, "Ever since he made the Fourth World, people can smile."

Thousands of children's voices have said and, a year later, continue to say, "We want to continue to bring children together; we want to take care of the poor."

"We are thinking a lot about Father Joseph."

"We must take on the responsibilities that Father Joseph held, trying to treat one another as equals."

"Father Joseph knew all about the happiness of unhappy children... All Taporis have to continue his work or make it known to people around them."

"To us Taporis, he was like the father of children with hard lives."

"Father Joseph was the best priest of all, and, anyway, he still is. He is still good, even though he is no longer with us."

"We will never forget him despite the fact that some did not know him like I did."

"God took him away. Father Joseph fulfilled his mission on earth. He has and he always will have an everlasting love. Father Joseph had a heart this big."

"We are promising him to fight against extreme poverty in spite of our sorrow. There will no longer be any famine, any drought or any inequality in the whole world and that is the finest homage that we can pay to Father Joseph. Thanks, Father Joseph, for having enabled me to understand."

"As for wars, human beings should understand and love one another. As for food, they should all be given some. That's what I wanted to tell you."

"I think that he will be very happy up there, especially if all of us continue to be Champions of Happiness."

In New York, Confesor Bracero, a Puerto Rican, and Tony Love, an African-American, are sitting in the lobby of a welfare hotel that takes in homeless families. They have not met Father Joseph in person, but they have just received a post card from him from Haiti. They take turns answering on a piece of cardboard: "God bless you. You are the finest person I have ever known. What can I say about such a nice person? I like you a lot. May God bless you.

This is coming to you from a very close friend. Tony." Both children participate in a street library that Father Joseph set up in New York. They belong to this Tapori Movement which, as a child, he created by urging his playmates from Saint-Jacques Street and from the Saint-Nicolas neighborhood "to be nice to parents who were too unhappy." Since he, himself, had been so unhappy about his childhood paths of shame, he never stopped opening paths of dignity and happiness to children squeezed together with their families, sometimes from seven to ten people in one room, in one of these welfare hotels, just as he did for children sleeping in the street, or under the marquee of a movie theater, or on a beach, or outdoors in an African city.

Not all children have the good fortune 14- and 15-year-old French students have of encountering him in a civics textbook. Even though his name is not yet "written in the dictionary," as little Marie wished, France now includes him in school curricula about human rights. Children from poor housing areas have found new pride in being able to say that it is indeed *their* Father Joseph who is being mentioned, "the same one who made the Fourth World and Taporis." We do not know who introduced Father Joseph into two textbooks, but whoever did helped to reconcile with school thousands of children from run-down housing areas.

## The Awakening Within the United Nations

This, then, is what children and adults, poor and non-poor, are saying, "We have to carry on." Many of them make a commitment through actions that are within their reach, such as the one we have just considered. Isn't Father Joseph himself perhaps continuing to "do what he has to do, up there," as one mother put it? Perhaps, "even though he's dead, he's thinking about us," as Maelle said? Volunteers who represent ATD Fourth World in international agencies sometimes feel they are meeting with him again on the way to offices and conference rooms where they used to accompany him.

In 1987, Father Joseph had pleaded one last time before the United Nations' Commission for Human Rights in favor of recognizing extreme poverty as a violation of human rights. He had came one last time before the Executive Board of UNICEF to ask it to recognize that the poorest among children were still excluded from

*Families from around the world at the Commemorative Stone in Paris, 1989.*

all its programs. In both places, Father Joseph spoke out in favor of a better knowledge of the facts and of a better understanding to be developed directly with the very poorest. It was still the same appeal, launched from the camp for homeless families in Noisy-le-Grand during the 1950s: "Let us get to know our poorest brothers and fellow citizens; let us treat them like real brothers and genuine partners."

In 1987, neither the Commission in Geneva, nor UNICEF in New York followed through. How then did it happen that, in these two international organizations, plagued by burning questions, everyone did not forget? On hearing the news of Father Joseph's death, the representative of the Argentinean government takes over in Geneva. He stands firm, in spite of refusals and snubs; he puts his job on the line. In New York, an upper-level civil servant takes charge of the project. By the time Volunteers launch another offensive in 1989 in both places, hearts and minds have changed. For the first time in the history of the United Nations, the very poor (not countries, but people — population groups) are going to become, for several days, the center of intense negotiations. An unexpected result, quite rare whenever poverty is concerned, is finally achieved: a resolution adopted by consensus!

In Geneva, governments of every political regime, both of rich and of developing countries, agree on the resolution, "Human Rights and Extreme Poverty." They recall "that international agreements concerning human rights recognize that the ideal of the free human being, freed from fear and chronic poverty, cannot be fulfilled unless conditions are established enabling all people to exercise their economic, social and cultural rights, as well as their civil and political rights." This was the language in which political leaders expressed what Father Joseph had been saying ever since 1956 in the Camp of Noisy-le-Grand: extreme poverty is a matter of human rights and human rights are indivisible. As Mr. Russel said, when speaking about the Wresinski Report in the People's University, "Everything has to be applied in order to eradicate extreme poverty. Eradicating extreme poverty means granting rights." The Commission put it in more technical terms: "The respect and promotion of human rights are indispensable in order to enable all people to participate in a free and responsible fashion in the development of the society in which they live." The Commission also vindicates Father Joseph and the families when it states that the world should strive to understand poverty better.

In New York, the Executive Board of UNICEF unanimously adopts the resolution, "Reaching the Poorest." The organization also recognizes what Father Joseph has been trying to tell the world for thirty years: "An important percentage of the world's population, including children and mothers, living in conditions of chronic poverty has not yet been reached by programs on behalf of the poor." The resolution also calls for more extensive knowledge. UNICEF is urged to work with the very poor through non-governmental organizations involved with them.

Government delegates seem all at once astonished by, and proud of, a decision for which no one had been given any mandate beforehand. For a short while, an exceptional atmosphere of brotherhood prevails among them. Some come over to hug representatives of the Movement in the middle of the session. In Geneva, two ambassadors from Latin America comment on the proceedings: "This is a double miracle," says one of them, a firm believer. The other, who no longer is, reflects, "Much remains to be done. We should ask Father Joseph to let us catch our breath for a while." To their minds, as to the minds of many, it is indeed Father Joseph's presence that continues to make itself felt. In fact, his presence seems to continue in many ways. Within those public spheres where Father Joseph was patiently moving forward, unexpected advances in awareness occur now that he has gone.

The Secretary General of the United Nations comes to the Commemorative Stone on the Plaza of Human Rights, by himself, as a friend. He talks with the families and makes a commitment to protect the International Volunteer Corps. The Director General of UNESCO agrees to sponsor all the Art and Poetry activities initiated by Father Joseph among extremely poor children on four continents. The Secretary General of the Council of Europe decides to meet with Tapori children every year and to publish officially what they expect from Europe. The European Economic and Social Committee, which never gave the Movement a hearing about poverty in the European Community, hosts a special session of the Fourth World People's University. More than one hundred Fourth World delegates hold their meeting inside its walls, discussing partnership on June 30, 1989. Did Father Joseph have to leave this world so that high ranking personalities might become aware of their responsibilities, as had many ordinary citizens, families and children? How did he manage, from beyond the grave, to unite the humble and the mighty in a common feeling that now is the time to commit oneself once and for all?

*Mr. Perez de Cuellar at the Commemorative Stone in Paris, 1989.*

**"Be United and Ready to Renounce the World."**

Is it true, perhaps, that "only a great love could accomplish this miracle," as a Volunteer put it? But who, then, will be able to understand and to carry on such a love that accomplishes miracles? It seems to us that it has shone through these pages, constantly defying our understanding, as we try to recount Father Joseph's life. What else can we do but pause in wonder and try to love as he did? What else can we do but try to trust as he did? "A great love can never be kept for oneself," Father Joseph said. Yet it cannot be shared only in words. We shall no doubt have to experience it fully together first, confident that we shall gain understanding as we move forward.

Father Joseph was convinced of this. He rarely talked about himself, since he was a humble man and since much of what he was living concerned only God. Only from time to time did he let us catch a glimpse. He never showed more than a glimpse, so as not to frighten us. One evening, with priests who were close friends, he evoked celibacy in these terms.

"A priest can reach complete fulfillment only by accepting to bear witness to his love of God by bearing insults, blows, injuries, and sometimes even death. For death is always a choice that a priest makes when he enters priesthood and gives himself over to the Lord. The acceptance of not having any offspring — in the face of a world that does not understand, in the face of Christians he will have to confront — is a sign of his acceptance of dying if he must, of disappearing. He accepts that his name be erased from the face of the earth, that it be forgotten among human beings so that it can be found again in God and that God alone remains in the memory of mankind."

The love Father Joseph refers to goes beyond human imagination. Yet his whole being, his entire life have indicated to us that he considered us all, rich or poor, humble or powerful, equally worthy and capable of such love. If not, would he have encouraged families harassed by extreme poverty to befriend families even more impoverished than themselves? Would he have suggested that, whatever our resources and our positions, we all share them with the most despised among people? Would he have wanted us to share them by loving to the point of becoming servants, slipping to the end of the line, making ourselves invisible, as he did over and over again himself? He did live among us, but with such discretion that we are discovering with dismay that, today, we can only guess at the depth of his inner life. *He* personified the priest to whom families owe their autonomy "because he left room for others... because he wanted respect not for himself but for others," ready to see his name erased from the face of the earth, to be found again in God. Is this not why many of us are looking for him now close to God? "Be ready to renounce the world," is what he was trying to teach us when he said, "Make yourselves inconspicuous, discreet and helpful; keep quiet; forget everything that you have learned in order to learn from them." Discretion is what he recommended to everyone across the board because, as ten-year-old Typhaine has understood, "everyone is the same, and no one is different."

Is there "a greater love than to give one's life to one's brothers" in exchange for the world's contempt? Father Joseph enabled everyone to grow. He reestablished unity among people by declaring all of them capable of such love; by building a movement where everyone can count on the determination of all the others to learn such selflessness. Could it be that the testimonies that fill these last pages confirm that he was not mistaken? Do they perhaps mean that he did not cast out his net into barren waters? He took God at his word. He relied on human beings, and the catch seems miraculous to us; miraculous for the Church, as an institution in any case. Didn't Monsignor Hardy say, on the day of his funeral, "Has Notre-Dame of Paris ever seen so many blackened hands, so many faces creased by life's pain and hardships, reach out toward the holy sacrament of the Eucharist?" But the catch was miraculous and unifying in another way as well.

"By not limiting his religious commitment to the Church as an institution, he reminded us that identification with the very poor goes beyond the institution." It is in these terms that Monsignor Charles Molette reflects about the unity Father Joseph was looking for. This unity is difficult to understand, since he was going after it without lengthy declarations, as if it were self-evident in the history of the very poor and of God, as well as, quite simply, in the history of mankind. "He presented the institution with the radical and total obligation of opening up beyond itself." Did he not, in fact, suggest this requirement to *every* institution, calling on women and men of *every* spiritual background to step outside of their walls, not only to join the very poor, but also to join together in a common service?

## "They Will Climb the Steps of the Church."

Fourth World families bear witness to this, they who were the first to understand this obligation, which Monsignor Molette calls radical and total. The unity that Father Joseph brought to them is fundamental in their eyes. Being united among themselves as families — from Bangkok, Manila, Dakar, Guatemala City, and a small protestant village in the Swiss mountains — gives them freedom, honor, and strength they would not have thought possible. They decide to go tell the Holy Father about this. For a long time, they had wanted to fulfill Father Joseph's dream that they would "climb the steps of the Vatican." Perhaps without realizing it yet, they had also set about preparing the fulfillment of that other ambition that was linked to it: "All my life, I have dreamed of giving the very poor back to the Church." We should remember that Father Joseph did not say to convert the very poor to the Church, but rather to give them back to the Church, so that they could teach her something essential about justice, freedom, and love; so that they could teach her their understanding of Jesus Christ as he walks through the Gospels, so that they could tell her about God living among them. He wanted to give the very poor back to the Church to strengthen her, but also to strengthen all of mankind in its certainty that each person is filled with the Holy Spirit and able to act on behalf of the world's well-being.

So, very poor families from four continents set out for Rome to talk about Father Joseph with the Pope and to tell him what this man meant to them. They asked the head of the Catholic Church what to do "so that Father Joseph would continue." They prepared themselves with seriousness for this meeting, and they were received with the seriousness that their history of suffering warranted.

"Father Joseph gives me one more reason for living, because, before I die, I want to see the dream of this more than wonderful man fulfilled," says Mr. Givart in Brussels. Participants in the People's University of Brussels carry on with this idea: "Father Joseph fought so that we would be less unhappy. He dared to meet more important people. Yet he taught us that it is not only the most important people who will be able to eradicate extreme poverty, but we ourselves as well... He was not afraid to go to large meetings and to say, 'What are you going to do for them?'" Father Joseph dared to do it; the families, in turn, are going to dare too. "This is my duty," says a Dutch mother. "We have to make up our minds, now."

But why do they decide to meet the Pope? "We could do with any church or any religion what we are doing with the Pope. Faith enables us to go in at any door, and this is the course we are now charting. We are carrying on what Father Joseph was not able to finish... Father Joseph taught us that poor people are not found in only one religion or one country, but rather that we must fight for them all. Father Joseph opened our hearts. We, the poorest people in Belgium, are not all alone; there are very poor people in the four corners of the earth... We are heading toward the Pope straight across the sea to promote kindness among all human beings. Through Father Joseph's work, we can go farther; we can build that huge house where everyone will be welcome."

The families are heading toward the Pope because all these things concern him. "The Pope, like Father Joseph, is for the poor; he is not only for the rich. We want him to know that, in our country, there are also poor people who want to honor him. This journey is important, even if afterwards we have to return to our lives of grinding hardships. Because we are going to tell the Pope that Father Joseph formed an alliance between all poor people — he who was poor himself and who knew what it meant to be poor and rejected. The Pope ought to bless us doubly now, so that we may be able to carry on. But he can also get in touch with other people and ask for their attention. The Pope must know that the very poor want to belong to the Church too. He has to convey this to the bishops and to all the priests."

In short, if the families went to Rome, it was because this was Father Joseph's Church, and because they love Father Joseph. Where else could they speak about him, tell about their sorrow at this separation, tell about their hope that he remain present but in this Church, which he called the place where he breathed? "The Pope is far away from us. We do not see him. We do not even know who he is or what his disposition and his intentions toward us are. How should we act when we meet him? But what does it matter? There are so many things to tell him about this priest, whose father he is, after all."

The families also have another reason to go to Rome. They want to do what Father Joseph has done with them, and what they have promised to continue, namely to bear witness to people even poorer than themselves, to families who are torn apart, evicted, and pursued, and about whom Father Joseph said one day that they were deprived of the right to inhabit the earth and even to exist. On four continents, families whose hands are useless in the eyes of the world are going to make a "Tapestry of Missing People." On bits of cloth, in the poor areas where they live, they embroider and recount the lives of families even more abandoned than themselves. So, the Tapestry, which represents Father Joseph's lifetime struggle, tells about a family in the Netherlands, evicted and condemned to go to a shelter where husband, wife, and even children are separated. It tells about a family living on a sidewalk in Bangkok whose parents have neither birth certificates nor passports and who will never be able to leave for a pilgrimage. (Although Buddhists, they had nonetheless dreamed of going to Rome.) The Tapestry also portrays a family in Africa that sought shelter in a cemetery from which it will be expelled sooner or later. This Tapestry, then, will also represent all families hiding in cemeteries on every continent; just as it will represent the many families who are afraid to go to Rome, fearing that their children will be taken from them, that their shanty will burn down or that the spot where they live under a sheet-metal roof will be taken over by squatters during their absence.

This is how we have "continued Father Joseph" — by working on a Tapestry: in a welfare hotel in New York, among squatters in a cemetery in Manila, in an inner courtyard in Lille, in a run-down district of Basel, on the public landfill of Guatemala City, and in a refuse container overlooking a city's rubbish pile where a family in a Dutch province found a dwelling place. Better yet, families in all these places have set out to "fulfill a dream" for him. Families from all cultural and religious backgrounds have prepared themselves for Rome. They have done so, filled with the anxiety of unending problems, facing the skepticism of their environment, yet determined to succeed. They never thought that Father Joseph's dreams were easy to fulfill. In their experience, it is above all major turning points in life that can call forth a thousand collaborations, a thousand inventions as yet unimagined. This is what happened with the gift to be offered to the Pope, which had to make him feel the presence of these millions of men, women, and children, driven away even from the dwelling places of poor people because their chronic poverty goes beyond anything imaginable. The "Tapestry of Missing People" was not their only gift. Families also dug up, collected, and skillfully enclosed earth from places of exile that had soaked up the sweat and the tears of the dispossessed: earth from a shantytown, from an uninhabitable and yet inhabited marsh, earth from a cemetery, earth from a slum that turns into sticky mud during the rainy season, parched earth where millet no longer grows, earth from a city dump where one has to dig deep to find any.

Scoop by scoop, families collected earth from areas of relentless poverty around the world, bearing witness to those whom the Pope would perhaps never see; bearing witness to this Father Joseph, "who was fighting for us." He knew that in each human being a message was swelling up and crying out. This message was: "We are alive, and we ask for the right to exist." "We cannot talk like Father Joseph," say the families who heard him on the Human Rights Plaza a certain October 17. The "I Bear Witness" address was delivered once and for all. Many of them keep this text among the important documents of their lives:

> I bear witness to you,
> the poor of all times
> still poor today,
> forever on the roads
> fleeing from place to place
> ...
> whose courage demands the right
> to priceless dignity...

Mr. Oorthuis hesitates a long time while considering his copy of the text, which he has folded and unfolded a thousand times to read to his neighbors, before saying, "I could offer this to the Holy Father." The same way Mr. and Mrs. Russel from Paris, Mr. Tempelaers from Antwerp, Mrs. Grün and Mrs. Fockeu from Liège have also spent a long time wondering how to convey to the Pope their conviction that Father Joseph had led the life of a saint and how to invite him to come to pray beside his tomb in Méry. To ensure that he becomes recognized fully in his Church, therefore, each and every one wants to be his ambassador.

All were confident that the Pope would understand, would support them and would speak to the world. Such was the unfathomable gift of a man who had come from the depths of extreme poverty to give back to his Church and the world the very poor, standing tall at last, confident and longing to be peace-makers,

*On July 27, 1989, the author led a delegation of 350 people to meet with Pope John Paul II. "Thanks to Father Joseph, you see before you parents whom the world, out of respect for you, keeps away from you out of a sense of decency, so as not to show you the lacerations of extreme poverty. Forbidden because of this to talk to you, they still wanted to come to see you."*

their hands filled with gifts. Such were the gifts placed at the feet of the Holy Father, in the courtyard of Castel Gandolfo, where the private audience lasted for an hour and a half, an audience during which the Pope listened, gave advice and made commitments. "If the Church, at times, may have given the impression of falling asleep in the presence of human misery, saints have arisen and have brought forth volunteers of evangelical love and solidarity with the poor... . I strongly encourage your Movement, which is certainly a worthy one, to consider and weigh the possibility of more developed or even new relations with the heads of individual Churches or with what we call the Bishops' Conferences." Saints have arisen and have brought forth volunteers... Go to the Church; the Church will look into matters with you... Fourth World families who, because of Father Joseph, dared "to climb the steps of his Church" have found their trust rewarded. In their opinion, "Father Joseph continues."

❖

"He died with us," families said last year. That was what you had wished for, Father Joseph: to plunge into the depths of poverty and to die with them. You had wished to see your name erased from the face of the earth, forgotten among the living so as to be found again in God. Our purpose is finding you again, wherever you are keeping watch now. "There are people whom you go on loving beyond death. That is how I feel with respect to Father Joseph," says Father Bach. "After his death, I said a mass for him here, on the very day when his body lay in Notre-Dame. I cannot forget him. He was a man who did so much good everywhere he went. An extraordinary man. My esteem and love for him cross the barrier of death, and we will see him again in glory."

"He is behind us; he is in front; we will see him again..." Families, friends, and Volunteers, we are walking toward him.

# SOURCES

— Wresinski, Father Joseph. *Les pauvres sont l'Eglise*. (Collection "Les Interviews"). Paris: Editions Le Centurion, 1983.

— Wresinski, Father Joseph. *Blessed Are You the Poor*!. Paris: Fourth World Publications, 1992. (Translation from the original French "*Heureux vous les pauvres*," Paris: Editions Cana, 1984.

— Wresinski, Father Joseph. *Les pauvres, rencontre du vrai Dieu*. Paris: Editions du Cerf / Science et Service-Quart Monde, 1986.

— Wresinski, Father Joseph. *Paroles pour demain*. Paris: Editions Desclée de Brouwer, 1986.

— Wresinski, Father Joseph. *Chronic Poverty and Lack of Basic Security*. French Economic and Social Council. Landover, MD.: Fourth World Publications, 1994. (Translation from the original French "*Grande pauvreté et précarité économique et sociale*." Originally published by the Journal of the Republic of France in 1987.)

— Wresinski, Father Joseph. *The Very Poor, Living Proof of the Indivisibility of Human Rights*. (Collection "Cahiers de Baillet.") Paris: Editions Quart Monde, 1994. (Translation from the original French "*Les plus pauvres, révélateurs de l'indivisibilité des Droits de l'homme*," Paris: La Documentation française, 1989.)

— Wresinski, Father Joseph and Alwine de Vos van Steenwijk. *Pologne, que deviennent tes sous-prolétaires?* Pierrelaye: Editions Science et Service-Quart Monde, 1981.

— Selected texts from the archives of the Joseph Wresinski House in Baillet-en-France.

# Photo Credits

**Page**

*FC* *(ATD Fourth World) Father Joseph, 1985.*

*BC* *(ATD Fourth World) The author with Father Joseph at the International Labor Organization, 1985.*

*3* *The Wresinski family, circa 1928. Joseph is on the left. "I learned everything from my mother."*

*11* *(ATD Fourth World) Rue Saint-Jacques in Angers. "The sun never got inside."*

*27* *Joseph, a seminarian, at the De Sessevalle mine.*

*43* *Father Joseph, circa 1957.*

*54* *(ATD Fourth World) The Camp of Noisy-le-Grand.*

*60* *(ATD Fourth World) An "igloo" in the Camp of Noisy-le-Grand. "No one could go outside without getting their shoes stuck in the mud."*

*63* *(A. Maclagan) Father Joseph in his office in Noisy-le-Grand, 1964.*

*66* *(ATD Fourth World) The chapel of the Camp of Noisy-le-Grand, built by Father Joseph in 1957.*

*66* *(ATD Fourth World) The interior of the chapel. Stained glass windows by Jean Bazaine. "Nothing is too beautiful for the poor."*

*70* *(ATD Fourth World) The laundry room in the Camp of Noisy-le-Grand, 1963.*

*76* *(A. Maclagan) Extreme poverty crosses all boundaries. Father Joseph with the author traveling to Cologne to visit emergency housing shelters for the homeless and to make new friends. Paris, 1961.*

*84* *(M. Marik) Mass on Christmas Eve in La Campa, 1968. "And it came to pass, in those days, that people decided to destroy shantytowns. They held a census of all the wretched of the earth who happened to be in shantytowns and rough-and-ready housing projects."*

*104* *(L. Prat) Father Joseph and others watch as bulldozers destroy shacks in the shantytown of La Campa, 1966.*

*105* *(G. Erpicum) With a family in the Val d'Oise, France, 1987.*

*108* *(United Nations) Javier Perez de Cuellar, then Secretary General of the United Nations, greets Father Joseph in 1984. "You are my eyes and ears in areas of extreme poverty in the world."*

*109* *(L. Prisset) Father Joseph leads a delegation of young people from four continents to see Pope John Paul II in 1982.*

*114* *(L. Prisset) Public lecture at the Sorbonne, "Defeating Persistent Poverty." Paris, 1983.*

*117* *(ATD Fourth World) Father Joseph in Noisy-le-Grand with a group of children in the early 1960s. "Among the thousands of children I have known, all of them held on to that innocence which refused to disappear, the wholesome outlook which could neither judge nor condemn."*

*121* *(J. Stadelmann) Philippines, 1987.*

*123 (M. Marik) J. and B. Jahrling's marriage, 1978.*

*126 (G. Erpicum) Senegal, 1987. Father Joseph writes in the guest book of Gorée Island, where people were held before being taken away as slaves.*

*138 (P. Leridant) Father Joseph's last People's University in Paris, 1987.*

*144 (J-P. Beyeler) Burkina Faso, 1986.*

*146 (L. Prisset) Father Joseph at a forum in Lille, France, 1983.*

*150 (R. Brustou) Cardinal Lustiger celebrates a funeral mass for Father Joseph in the Cathedral of Notre-Dame of Paris on February 18, 1988.*

*153 (ATD Fourth World) The chapel in Méry-sur-Oise, France, where Father Joseph was laid to rest. 1989.*

*156 (ATD Fourth World) Father Joseph's tomb, 1989.*

*162 (M. Marik) Pierrelaye, France, 1981. Father Joseph welcomes participants to the Seminar on "Extreme Poverty and Exclusion in Africa." "We had experienced such loneliness for a long time that we promised one another to look for people who, like you, are facing extreme poverty by themselves."*

*163 (G. Erpicum) Guatemala, 1985.*

*170 (ATD Fourth World) With children in Reunion Island, 1981.*

*173 (ATD Fourth World) Families from around the world at the Commemorative Stone in Paris, 1989.*

*175 (ATD Fourth World) Mr. Perez de Cuellar at the Commemorative Stone in Paris, 1989.*

*182 (E. Mandelmann) On July 27, 1989, the author led a delegation of 350 people to meet with Pope John Paul II. "Thanks to Father Joseph, you see before you parents whom the world, out of respect for you, keeps away from you out of a sense of decency, so as not to show you the lacerations of extreme poverty. Forbidden because of this to talk to you, they still wanted to come to see you."*